How to Train a
Guard Dog

by John Larson

P.O. Box 14, Rosemead, CA 91770

© 1987 by J. Flores Publications

All rights reserved. Reproduction in whole or in part without written permission from the publisher is strictly prohibited.

Neither the author nor the publisher assumes any responsibility for the use or misuse of any information contained in this book.

ISBN 0-918751-05-5

Library of Congress Catalog Card No. 86-81033

Printed in the United States of America

Cover photo courtesy of:
Sunnydae Kennels
George & Pam Higgins
29586 N. Gossell Rd
Wauconda, IL 60084
(312) 526-3499

TABLE OF CONTENTS

Introduction	7
Should you Train your Own Dog?	9
Which Breed Should you Choose for Defensive Use?	12
Safety	15
Diseases and Their Prevention	17
Inspecting and Grooming your Dog	30
First Aid	40
Feeding	49
Behavior and Motivation	54
Training Equipment	63
Principles of Dog Training	69
Obedience Training	73
Intermediate Training	96
Advanced Training	100

Introduction

Recently, a burglar tried to break into the house of one of my friends. Having jumped over the back yard fence, he was heading towards a back window, when all of a sudden my friend's German Shepherd jumped him. How he managed to escape we'll never know, as traces of blood were found all over the yard and on the street.

Examples of dogs preventing crimes such as this are becoming increasingly common as more people realize the potential of these animals as crime stoppers and defensive allies.

Law-enforcement agencies and the military have known this for many years. They have developed most training methods to take advantage of the dog's intelligence and loyalty.

Although the use of police and military dogs may be traced as far back as the reign of Pyrrhus, King of Epirus (295-272 BC), it was following the Korean War that state-of-the-art development in canine behavior and training really took off.

This, coupled with a spiraling crime rate at home, rekindled interest in defensive working dogs, especially in jurisdictions where on-the-street crimes were reaching epidemic proportions. By 1970, over 80 police departments were employing dogs as part of their patrol force. Today the rate is much higher.

The Vietnam Conflict produced major developments in the employment and effectiveness of military dogs. As many as 1,700 dogs of all types were actively engaged in support of all services. In addition to the proven sentry and scout dogs, the requirements of the war produced the mine/tunnel detection dog, the combat tracker and marijuana detector dogs. Development of off-leash techniques gave increased range and warning ability.

An important outgrowth of the conflict was the development of canine research and development efforts. These ongoing efforts were able to initiate the first steps toward developing a more intelligent and stronger security dog; training dogs to detect specific drugs and explosives; developing multiple-purpose dogs; and employment of tactical dogs by electronic remote control.

For the civilian, these new training techniques mean that now he too can have a dog able not only to protect property, but his life as well.

Should you Train your Own Dog?

There are no purely objective methods of determining how well a prospective trainer qualifies in the desirable traits of a dog handler.

To successfully care for and train dogs, you must possess certain characteristic traits such as proper attitude, patience and perseverance, mental and physical coordination, resourcefulness, dependability, and physical endurance.

Friendly attitude toward dogs

If you choose to train your own dog, you must have a genuine fondness for and interest in dogs.

Patience and perseverance

You cannot force desired behavior upon dogs, nor can you expect them to learn as rapidly as human beings. Don't be disturbed by a dog's apparent inability to correctly accomplish a feat. Don't lose your temper easily. Accept the fact that dogs must be taught slowly and that most exercises must be repeated often before they learn to execute certain tasks properly.

Mental and physical coordination

You must be able to convey your wishes to your dog by gestures as well as voice. This requires a large amount of mental and physical coordination. Vocal commands must be clear and concise. When necessary, hand signals or gestures must be given simultaneously with vocal commands.

Resourcefulness

Although most training procedures are carefully set forth, situations will arise which call for actions not covered by any set rules. To be a successful trainer, you must recognize these situations and be able to improvise means with which to control them.

Rules for training dogs are designed to apply to most dogs, however, no two dogs are exactly alike with regard to their characteristics and their ability to learn. Because of this, established rules for training and handling may be adopted to fit the needs of the individual animal.

Dependability

The welfare of the dog is entirely in your hands. Dogs can't disclose how they are being treated. Their physical well-being depends primarily on your willingness to do such manual labor as necessary regarding feeding and cleanliness.

Physical endurance

Not only must you be able to show good coordination; but you must be able to maintain your efforts as long as necessary. A trainer must be able to "out-last" his dog during each training period.

Which Breed Should you Choose for Defensive Use?

Any breed of dog could be trained for defensive uses. However, the breed that has been selected over others by police and military organizations the world over has been the German Shepherd. This breed has the best combination of characteristics necessary for defensive use. Of course, if you already have a dog and want to train it for defensive use there should be no problems.

Characteristics

One of the most important characteristics of the German Shepherd is its ability to adapt to different climatic conditions.

The breed has a double coat of hair, the outer coat is long, coarse, and somewhat water resistant. The undercoat is soft and furry, and grows thick when the weather or climate is cold.

The German Shepherd has a long tireless gaint. It is strong, alert, fearless and agile. It is not a vicious animal, however, it has a natural distrust of strange persons or situations.

Specifications

Dogs chosen for defensive work should conform to the following specifications.

1) The dog must be sturdy and compact.
2) It must reveal evidence of power, endurance and energy.
3) The dog may be of either sex, but females should be spayed.
4) The animal should be at least 23 inches in height.
5) The dog's weight should be at least 60 pounds.
6) It should be between 12 and 36 months of age.
7) It should have good muscle tone, clear eyes and an alert attitude.
8) The outer coat should be dense. The undercoat varies in density with the season of the year and with the geographical region.
9) A dog with minor breed defects (coarse or domed head, hanging ears, tail defect and the like) can still be used.
10) A male which has been castrated or which has one or both testicles undescended is acceptable.
11) The dog must have strong teeth, but not more than four may be missing. None of the missing teeth may be a canine tooth. A dog with serious erosion of the enamel of its teeth or with badly worn teeth should not be used.
12) Do not use a dog with an overshot or undershot jaw.

Temperament

An acceptable dog must show evidence of alertness, aggressiveness, steadiness, vigor and responsiveness. A timid, shrinking or cowardly animal is not acceptable and shouldn't be used.

State of health

In conjunction with the temperament and physical soundness of the dog, its overall state of health must be considered. An animal must be in good health. The best way to find out is to take it to a veterinarian. Have him give your dog a complete check-up.

The dog should be tested for signs of heartworms, defective sense of hearing, vision or smell. It should also be checked for signs of bone or joint disease. These diseases impair the ability of the animal to perform to its maximum potential.

The following breeds are recommended for defensive use.
1) German Shepherd
2) Labrador Retriever
3) Dobermann
4) Boxer
5) Pitt Bull Terrier
6) Siberian

Test for suitable temperament

This test determines whether your dog responds appropriately to mild agitation. To perform this test, someone approaches the dog and strikes at it with a rolled magazine or some other harmless device. The dog should respond by growling, barking, or attempting to bite the agitator.

Some dogs, when initially exposed to mild agitation, will be startled for a few seconds and may appear frightened. This response should not cause a dog to be disqualified for training. If, however, the animal repeatedly acts frightened by the agitator it is unsuitable for training.

Safety

You must learn good safety habits and practice them at all times. Some people believe that defensive or "guard" dogs, whether on leash or loose, are walking safety hazards. A safety conscious person can prevent dogs from committing unsafe acts and thereby dispel such misconceptions.

Whether you keep your dog in the yard or inside the house (not recommended), refrain from running or engaging in any type of "horseplay". Such actions tend to stimulate dogs and could create a situation wherein the animal might run and cause injury to itself, a person, or another animal.

Use caution to maintain control of your dog when moving it from one place to another. Grasp the leash so that it remains close to you. A leash can be shortened sufficiently by securing the loop of the leash to your right wrist and placing your left hand on the leash with the knuckles facing upward. Don't place your hand directly on the snap.

Safety precautions

The following are some of the specific safety precautions that should always be observed.
1) Secure all doors and gates. If your dog escapes to the street, you could be held liable for any damage.
2) Always keep your dog on a leash when out of the house.
3) Learn to recognize signs which indicate that a dog is preparing to bite. Such signs include growling, curling lips or baring teeth, staring and standing perfectly still, and rising hackles on neck.
4) Never kick, slap, or hit your dog.

Diseases and Their Prevention

Contagious diseases of dogs

A contagious disease is one which can be transmitted or spread from one animal to another. Some of the contagious diseases of dogs can be spread not only from one dog to another but also to humans.

This section emphasizes your responsibilities in improving your dog's health. It's impractical to present here all the many diseases which can affect dogs, therefore, only the most common and serious are discussed.

Canine distemper

This is a widespread viral disease. It is a very serious, highly contagious disease, which is often fatal. It is very common, with puppies and non-vaccinated dogs being most susceptible.

An infected animal may show the following signs: yellowish discharge from the eyes and nose, coughing, fever, loss of appetite, loss of vitality, diarrhea and convulsions. Vaccination is an extremely important and effective method of controlling canine distemper.

Infectious canine hepatitis

This is also a widespread viral disease among dogs, and, as with distemper, it is seen most commonly in young dogs but may affect animals of all ages. The majority of infected animals recover after a long period of recuperation.

Infectious canine hepatitis is spread from one animal to another through contaminated feeding and drinking pans and through the urine from infected dogs. This virus primarily affects the blood vessels of the liver.

Signs of the disease resemble those of distemper in many cases, and it is often difficult to distinguish between the two. The most prominent symptoms are fever, loss of vitality, and loss of appetite. Be sure to immunize your dog against this disease.

Rabies

This disease, also called Hychrophobia, is one of the most serious diseases of men and animals. It is caused by a virus. Some countries of the world are free of the disease, but in most—including the United States—it is still a problem.

Rabies is spread by the saliva of infected animals. For this reason, it is usually associated with the bite from an infected animal. All warm-blooded animals may be infected by this disease, and most infected animals die.

In the United States, some of the animals most frequently affected are skunks, raccoons, bats, foxes, dogs, cattle and cats. In an animal with rabies, the nerves, spinal cord and brain are the parts of the body most affected.

Signs of rabies may include a sudden change of disposition, excitement, difficulty in swallowing water or food, paralysis and coma.

Dogs with rabies often have a paralysis of the muscles in the jaw and the lower jaw remains partially dropped. Such an animal may appear to have something lodged in the mouth or throat. It is always wise for you to have an animal with such symptoms examined by a veterinarian, rather than attempt an examination yourself.

There are many other types of contagious diseases which may affect your dog. Have your veterinarian administer all necessary vaccinations. Your dog should also be given a medical examination at least once a year.

Leptospirosis

This disease is caused by spiral micro-organisms of the genus leptospira, and it is fairly common in dogs. Animals other than dogs can also be infected, and it can be transmitted to man. It is a serious disease and many infected dogs die. Leptospirosis is spread through the urine of infected animals; dogs and rats are common sources of infection.

Signs may include muscular stiffness and soreness, fever, reddening of the membranes of mouth and eyes, loss of appetite, vomiting and diarrhea. As with distemper and infectious canine hepatitis, immunization is the method used to prevent the disease.

To control the spread of leptospirosis, the kennel area must be kept free of rats, and the food and water supply must be protected from contamination by urine from infected dogs. The possibility of human infection points out the need for personal hygiene when handling dogs. Since there are several diseases which can be passed from dog to man, you must always wash your hands thoroughly after handling your dog.

In localities in which leptospirosis is known or suspected to exist dogs should not be allowed to unnecessarily enter streams, rivers or other bodies of water since they may be contaminated from the urine of infected animals.

Parasitic infections

Parasites that live on the outside of a host's body are called external parasites. Those that live inside the body are called internal parasites. Many of these live in the intestines, and one type lives in the dog's heart.

All parasites are harmful to the health of the animal, and some can spread diseases to the dog or to yourself. Parasites should be controlled as much as possible. Consult your veterinarian as to the best way to handle specific cases.

When speaking of parasites, the term "life cycle" refers to the stages of development in the parasite's life from its beginning as an egg or larva (immature form) to the time it becomes an adult. A knowledge of the life cycle is important in the control of parasites (see illustrations).

External parasites

External parasites are all small insects. These parasites, which live on and in the skin, cause damage by sucking blood or by feeding on the dog's tissues. In doing so, they produce an irritation, and the dog responds by biting and scratching itself.

Examples of external parasites include:

Ticks

These small parasites are common in many parts of the world; they suck the blood from the animal and, when present in large numbers, may cause a serious anemia. Ticks can often be observed standing still on the dog's body with their heads buried deep in the skin. Through their bites, ticks are important vectors of disease producing agents, such as bacteria and rickettsiae in animals as well as man. Exercise care when handling ticks and request instructions from the veterinarian before trying to remove them.

Ticks do not necessarily spend all of their lives on the body of the dog. They may be found in bedding, carpeting, or in cracks in the floors and sides of the kennel; they may be present in grass and bushes. Control, therefore, does not depend only on treating the individual animal. It may also be necessary to treat the kennels and training and working areas with insecticides. Treatment with insecticides must be accomplished only with the approval of a veterinarian, as many chemicals can be dangerous to the health of the animal.

Fleas

These pests torment the dog, irritate the skin, and spread disease; they are most often observed as they crawl or hop very rapidly through the dog's coat of hair. They are very difficult to control because they do not spend all their time on the body but live in bedding and in the cracks of the kennel. Control depends upon repeated individual treatment and kennel sanitation. Use flea powders and collars to keep this problem under control.

Lice

There are two types of lice which affect dogs: biting lice and sucking lice. Biting lice live off the dog's tissues; sucking lice suck the animal's blood. Both produce great irritation. Biting lice may be observed crawling over the skin and through the hair. When feeding, sucking lice are usually immobile and attach themselves so that they are perpendicular to the skin of the host.

The eggs of lice are called nits and are found as small white or gray crescent shaped objects fastened to the hairs. Lice, unlike fleas and ticks, can live only a short time when they are not on the dog's body. Control, therefore, depends more on the treatment of affected animals.

Mites

There are several types of small parasites called mites which affect dogs and produce a condition known as mange. One of these, the ear mite, lives in the ear canals and causes severe irritation. Affected dogs not only scratch at the ears but may hold their heads to one side and frequently shake their heads. The ear canals usually contain a large amount of dark-colored discharge.

Ear mites are small but visible to the naked eye as tiny white crawling specks. Most of the other mites which affect the dog live on the animal's skin, but one lives in the nasal passages. These mites are too small to be seen with the naked eye and can be seen only with the aid of a microscope.

Internal parasites

The parasites which live in the body may cause damage by irritating the tissues, by constantly robbing the body of blood or essential parts of the diet, or by interfering with a specific body action.

Examples of internal parasites include:

Hookworms

One of the most harmful parasites that lives in the dog's intestines is the hookworm. These parasites are small and threadlike, only 1/3 to 4/5 of an inch in length. They suck blood and also cause blood loss by grasping and tearing at the intestinal wall with the many teeth in their mouths.

The adult lives in the dog's intestine, and eggs are produced by the female hookworms. The eggs are passed in the infected dog's feces. Immature hookworms (larvae) develop from these eggs, and these larvae can then infect the same or another dog. The larvae gain entrance to the body by penetrating the dog's skin or by being swallowed as the dog licks the ground or itself.

After the larvae gain entrance to the body, they pass directly to the intestine or migrate through the body tissues to the lungs. Those reaching the lungs are coughed up and swallowed, thereby reaching the intestine. Once they are in the intestine, they develop into adult hookworms and the life cycle begins again.

Dogs infected with hookworms may have a variety of symptoms, depending on the severity of the infection. Membranes of the mouth and eyes may be pale; feces may be loose and contain blood; the animal may lose weight. The veterinarian makes a diagnosis of the disease when, by microscopic examination, he finds hookworm eggs in the animal's feces.

Control measures consist of treating the individual animal and, to a large extent, on good sanitation. The handler who has a knowledge of the hookworm's life cycle should understand the importance of keeping the kennel area and training ground free of feces, since feces from infected animals are the source of infection.

Roundworms

These adult parasites also live on the intestine. They are much larger than hookworms and vary in length from 2 to 8 inches. Adult roundworms cause trouble by depriving the affected animal of essential nutrients in the diet. The life cycle is similar to that of the hookworm but the eggs do not develop into larvae until swallowed. They then enter the blood stream and migrate to such organs as the liver, kidney, and lungs, producing great damage in the process. Most finally reach the lungs where they are coughed up and swallowed to return to the intestine to mature.

Symptoms shown by an infected animal may include vomiting, diarrhea, loss of weight, and coughing. As with hookworms, the diagnosis is made by finding the eggs in the feces; occasionally, adult worms may be vomited or passed in the feces, in which case you may be able to see them.

Whipworms

These intestinal parasites are much smaller than roundworms but larger than hookworms. The life cycle is different from that of the hookworms and roundworms in that the whipworm larvae do not enter the blood stream or migrate to other organs; they mature in the intestine of the dog. Symptoms of infection may include diarrhea, loss of weight, and paleness of the membranes of the mouth and eyes.

The diagnosis is made by microscopic observation of the characteristic eggs in the feces.

Tapeworms

These worms are long, flat, and ribbonlike in appearance. They have many segments and a head. The tapeworm uses its head to attach itself to the wall of the intestine. Several kinds of tapeworms may infect the dog's intestine; only the most common one is described here. The life cycle of the tapeworm is rather complex. After the proglotteds with eggs have passed in the dog's feces, they are eaten by the larvae (immature form) of the dog flea, the external parasite previously described. The larva of the tapeworm develops in the flea; and when the adult flea is eaten by a dog, the tapeworm larva gains entrance to the animal's intestines where it develops into an adult tapeworm. The symptoms produced by tapeworms may not be too noticeable. They may include diarrhea, loss of appetite, and loss of weight.

Some tapeworms pass through the bodies of rabbits, mice, or squirrels (instead of the flea) during their life cycle. Dogs become infected by eating a rabbit or other animal which contains the tapeworm larvae. Often the eggs of the tapeworm cannot be detected by the veterinarian during feces examinations. Many times, however, segments may be seen in the feces or among the hairs in the dog's anal region. They are small white objects about 1/4 of an inch long and they may be moving in a rhythmic manner.

Control measures include treatment of the infected animal, good sanitation in the kennel area, control of fleas, and not allowing the dog to eat animals which are likely sources of infection.

Heartworms

Unlike the other internal parasites that have been described, the adult heartworm is found in the heart and lungs rather than in the intestine. This parasite interferes with the dog's heart action and circulation. The adult worms are threadlike in appearance and are from 6 to 11 inches long.

The adult worms in the heart produce larvae which are called microfilariae. These microfilariae circulate in the infected animal's blood stream where they may be picked up by mosquitoes, the insect responsible for the spread of the heartworm parasite from one dog to another. The larvae continue their development in the mosquito and then after a period of time are introduced into the dog's tissues as the mosquito is biting. The microfilariae mature and then travel to the heart of the dog and develop into adults; the life cycle is ready to begin again.

Dogs infected with heartworms may exhibit coughing, loss of weight, difficult breathing, and a loss of stamina. The disease is diagnosed by the veterinarian when he finds microfilariae during a blood test. Treatment is then given to kill the adult worms and the microfilariae. Control measures consist of treating and quarantining infected dogs to prevent them from serving as sources of infection, and of controlling mosquitoes in the area. Treatment of infected dogs includes kennel rest of up to 6 months.

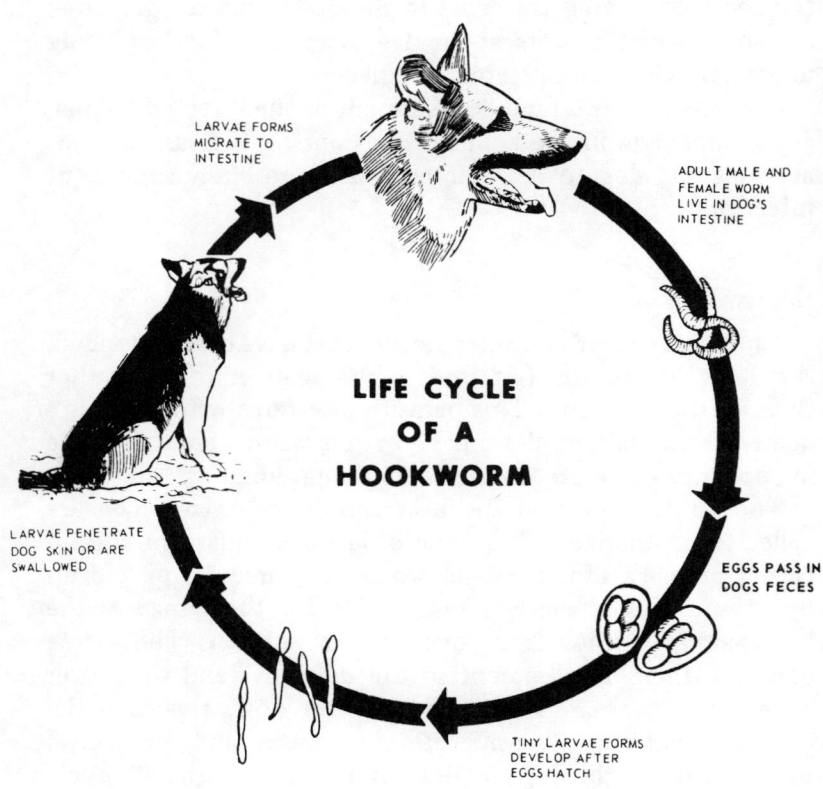

Life cycle of hookworm.

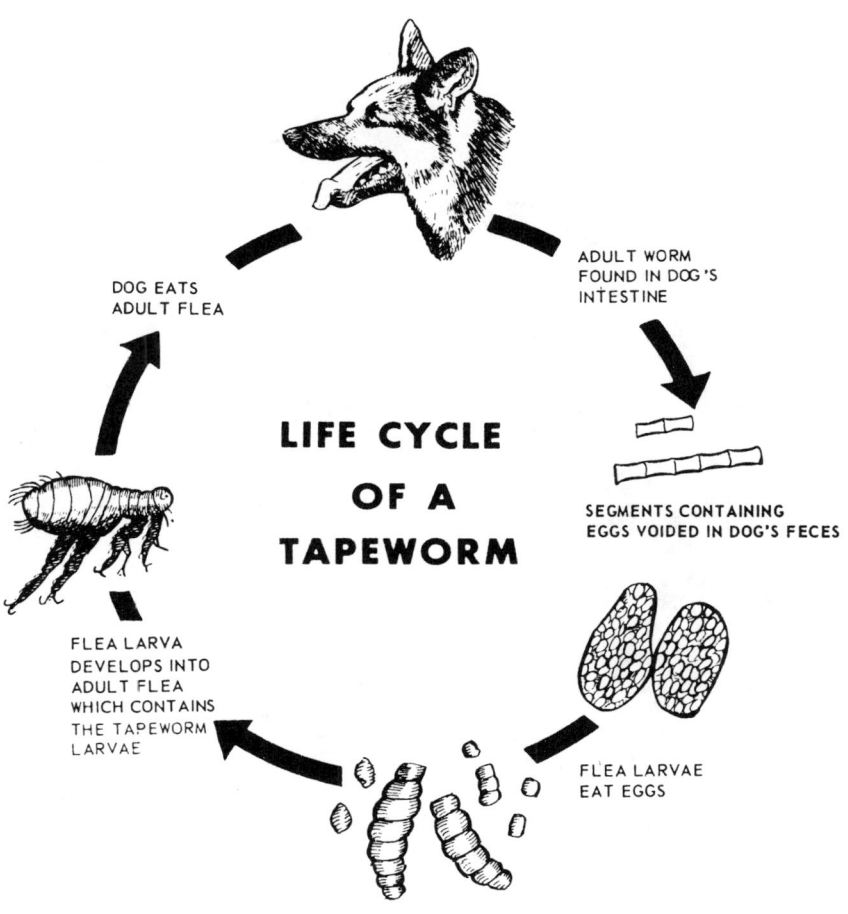

Life cycle of tapeworm.

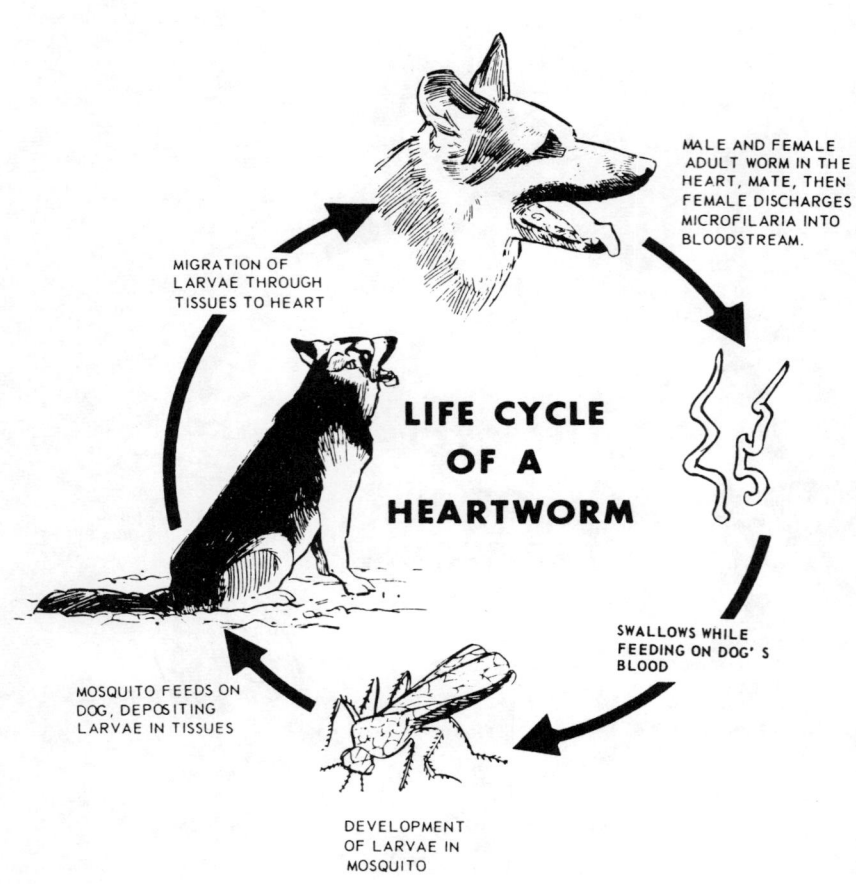

Life cycle of heartworm.

Sanitation

Cleanliness is one of the most important factors contributing to the good health of dogs. Practice sanitary measures at all times, as a good standard of cleanliness must be maintained.

Disease control and sanitation cannot be separated, and there are many specific ways in which a good level of sanitation can be maintained.

Food prepared or served with dirty hands or in dirty utensils is a source from which your dog may contract some disease. To prevent disease, clean and sanitize the food and water pans daily. Clean the utensils used in the preparation of food immediately after each food preparation period.

One particular piece of equipment which must be cleaned is the can opener. Clean the blade everytime you use it. Store food in rat-proof areas so that dry meal or cans are not soiled by rat urine or stools.

Sweep the kennel daily if possible, and scrub it at least once a week, more often if necessary.

The areas around the kennel must also be maintained clean. Remove feces from this area daily, as this is a common source of infection in the spread of disease. In the entire kennel area there must be no accumulation of refuse and garbage which would attract rats and insects.

In regions where mosquitoes are a problem, control measures should be taken to control them. Several kinds of disinfectants can be used around a kennel area. They can be used to disinfect feeding pans, kennels and adjacent areas.

Inspecting and Grooming your Dog

Routine grooming and inspection are important events in the life of a defensive dog—so important in fact that they should be accomplished if possible on a daily basis the year round.

You must realize that grooming is essential to the proper care of the dog's skin and coat of hair.

During inspection of your dog, look for signs of illness or disease which may be affecting the health of the animal. A large part of the inspection is performed while the dog is being groomed.

The daily grooming and inspection period should be a pleasant experience for both you and your dog. This is the time when the two of you can relax while doing something useful together. The dog looks forward to its grooming, and you know that you are contributing directly to the fulfillment of your responsibility for its health.

Grooming

To groom the dog, first give it a brisk rubdown with the fingertips moving against the grain, then rub with the grain to remove hair. This loosens any dead skin, hair, or dirt and brings it to the surface. It also massages the skin.

Follow the rubdown with a thorough but gentle brushing against the grain, to remove the loosened skin, hair and dirt. Next, brush the coat with the grain; this returns the hair to its natural position.

Finally, rub the coat with the palms of the hands with the grain of the hair. This helps distribute the oil and gives the coat a glossy appearance. Occasionally, comb the dog's coat, but in winter combing should be limited to avoid tearing out the warm undercoat.

Bathing is not a part of routine grooming, but occasionally a bath may be needed. A dog's skin has many glands which produce an oily substance; this oily substance keeps the skin soft and prevents it from drying and cracking. In addition, it protects the coat of hair and makes it water repellant. When a dog is bathed too often, the natural oil is removed, and the skin and hair become unnaturally dry, resulting in skin problems.

Rely on the advice of a veterinarian as to the frequency of bathing, the type of soap to use, and how to protect your dog's eyes and ears. A thorough rinsing after the bath is important. If soap is left in the coat it becomes sticky, collects dirt, and may cause skin irritation.

Dry the animal with a towel or suitable substitute. After it has been dried as thoroughly as possible, the dog may be gently exercised in the sun to complete the drying. Do not bathe a dog in cold or wet weather unless it can remain in a warm place until completely dry.

Inspection

Routine daily inspection is a part of, but by no means limited to, the grooming and inspection period. During each grooming period make it a habit to take the time to check over each part of your dog's anatomy for signs or symptoms of illness or injury. After you've had your dog for some time, you will know what it should look like, and how it should act when healthy and well.

You know what is normal for your dog: how its coat of hair looks, how many bowel movements it has a day, and how much it eats every day. When making this daily inspection, use this knowledge to detect anything abnormal about the animal.

For example, the animal may not have eaten all of its food for a day or two. It may have an area of hair loss and reddened skin somewhere on the body, or it may have a discharge coming from the nose.

If you notice anything abnormal about the appearance or actions of your dog, report it immediately to your veterinarian. Do not attempt to diagnose the illness and apply home remedies, which can often do more harm than good. Rely on the veterinarian who is trained to provide expert medical care for the animal.

The veterinarian depends on you to detect and report any symptoms of illness or injury. Early detection is important. If treatment begins early, there is a better chance for a rapid and complete recovery.

Learn the terms used to describe the various parts of a dog's external anatomy. This will enable you to read intelligently about your dog, to report symptoms of illness or injury accurately, and to understand the veterinarian's instructions for treatment.

During inspections, it's necessary that you check specific places on the animal for symptoms of disease or injury.

Eyes

The dog's eyes are often referred to as the mirror of its body. This means that illness of the body is often accompanied by changes in the eyes. In addition, many illnesses affect only the eyes.

Normally, a dog's eyes are bright and clear. The surrounding membranes should be a healthy pink in color. The small wedge-shaped membrane at the inner corner of the eyes is known as the nicitating membrane or the third eyelid. Normally this covers only a very small part of the inner portion of the eye.

Look for any of the following symptoms: A reddish or yellowish discoloration of the membranes of the eyes, the presence of whitish or yellowish discharges from the eyes, and cloudiness or other discoloration of the clear portion of the eyes (cornea).

Other symptoms to watch for are puffiness of the lids, lids held partially or completely closed, or the nicitating membranes covering more than the normal part of the cornea. Be careful not to injure the dog's eyes when examining them.

Nose

The black pad at the end of a dog's nose is usually shiny and moist. If it is persistently dry and dull, this may be a symptom of illness.

Other symptoms to look for: the presence of a watery, yellowish, or red-tinged discharge coming from or caked around the external openings of the nose, sneezing, snorting, and pawing at the nose. Do not, under any circumstance, probe into the dog's nose with any object.

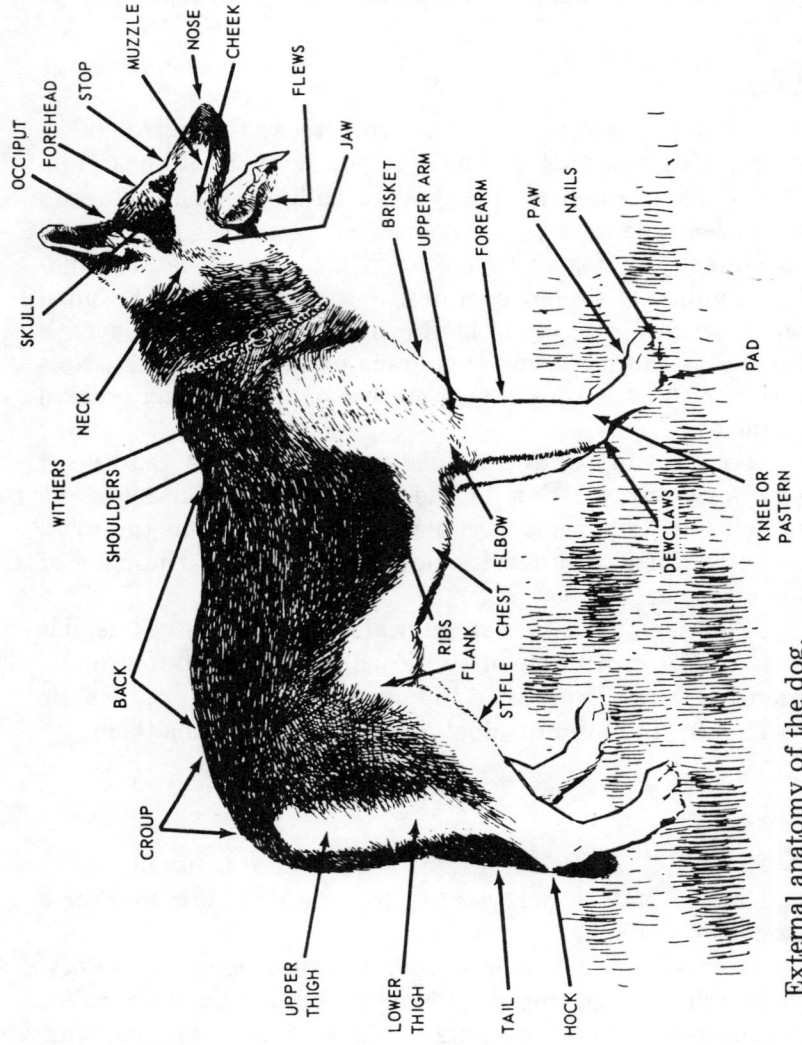

External anatomy of the dog.

Ears

The erect external portion of the ear is called the ear flap. Leading downward from the base of the ear flap is the ear canal. The portion of the canal which can be seen with the naked eye is known as the vertical canal. The deeper portion, which cannot be seen, is the horizontal canal. Small quantities of brownish wax are frequently seen in the vertical canal and are normal. The presence of a reddish discoloration, swelling, or large amounts of discharge in the ear canal are abnormal and should be checked with the veterinarian.

Other symptoms to report include: a foul odor coming from the canals, shaking of the head, drooping of one or both ears, holding the ear flap down, holding the head to one side, twitching the ear, scratching or pawing at the ear, and evidence of pain when the ear is touched.

Mouth

When you look into the dog's mouth, numerous things should be checked. Normally, the gums and inner aspect of the lips are salmon pink. The teeth are firm and shiny white in color.

Symptoms of illness to look for include paleness of the gums and membranes, redness and bleeding of the gums, sores of various types, persistent drooling, bloody saliva, and a foul breath.

Loose or broken teeth, tartar accumulations on the teeth, and foreign objects lodged between the teeth are other conditions to watch out for. Also notice any gagging or pawing at the mouth.

Skin and hair coat

Under normal conditions, the hair coat has a glossy appearance. If the dog is well fed and groomed, the skin should be soft and pliable.

The hair coat is subject to changes in appearance when the climate or seasons change. The undercoat is thicker and more prominent in cold climates or seasons. Shedding is more noticeable in hot climates. These changes in the dog's coat are normal.

The following conditions are indications of skin trouble: reddening, scabbing, moist discharges, scratching, shedding that is unusual for the season or climate, loss of hair in one or several spots, dryness, and loss of pliability.

Always watch for fleas, ticks, and lice. Frequently these insects and parasites are first noticed around the ears, at the back of the neck, along the backbone, and around the tail and anal regions.

Feet

Proper care and attention must be given to the feet if the animal is to carry out its duties effectively. Inspect the dog's feet for foreign objects that may be caught in the pads or hair, for cuts and bruises, and for abrasion of the pads.

The dog usually keeps its nails worn to the proper length so the tips of the nails do not touch the ground when it stands. Sometimes, however, the nails become so long they can interfere with the dog's work. Pay particular attention to the nails on the dewclaws since they are not worn down by contact with the ground and may grow until they curve back into the legs. Note any lameness shown by the animal because this may indicate a foot problem.

Limbs

Carefully check the legs of your dog, as well as the feet. Wounds, swellings, and sores of various kinds may be found. On the forelegs opposite the outer part of the elbow there may develop an area of hairless, thickened skin known as a callus. This is an area about an inch in diameter. When the dog lies down or gets up, a pressure and abrasive action are exerted on the callus, and it may become inflamed. If this happens report it to the veterinarian.

Genitals

If the dog is a male, there are certain things to look for in the genital organs. The penis is located in a fold of skin known as the prepuce or sheath. Normally, a small amount of greenish-yellow discharge comes from the prepuce which the dog removes while cleaning itself. If this discharge is present in excessive amounts report it to a veterinarian.

The penis is subject to a variety of **injuries**. Report immediately the appearance of blood from the **prepuce**. The scrotum is the pouch of skin in which the testicles are located. Note any swelling, reddening, or scabbing of the scrotum.

In the female dog, the external opening of the genital tract is called the vulva. Normally, there is no discharge from the vulva. Reddening of the vulva, or of the skin in the area, and a discharge from the vulva should be reported to the veterinarian.

Anal region

The last portion of the dog's digestive tract is called the rectum, and the opening from the rectum to the outside of the body is called the anus. On either side of the rectum near the anus is a small gland known as the anal gland. These especialized glands, which secrete a brownish, foul-smelling substance, have a sac called the anal sac. Sometimes, the opening of the sac gets clogged and becomes swollen and painful.

Look for any swelling and reddening of the skin in the area of the anus itself. When the anal glands need to be emptied or are infected, the dog may turn to bite at the area, or may slide along the ground while in a sitting position. Report any of these symptoms to your veterinarian.

Attitude

Your dog's attitude is one of the best indications of its general state of health. Through close association with and knowledge of your dog, you can readily detect a change of attitude.

If a dog tires easily or begins to show undue nervousness, loss of vitality and energy, an increased desire for sleep, or inattention while training, there may be something wrong with it.

Body functions

This refers to the natural functions which are continuously carried on by the body: breathing, digestion, formation of waste products, and the like. Disturbances in these natural functions are accompanied by many symptoms. Alertness in detecting them is important.

Notice any increase or decrease in appetite or thirst, or any change in the manner of breathing, such as an unusual amount of panting. Vomiting may occur, or there may be a change in the nature of the intestinal contents as evidenced by a very soft or watery feces. Blood may be seen in the vomiting or feces.

Whenever possible, watch the dog when it starts urinating or having a bowel movement. By doing so, you may be able to detect blood in the urine or to detect that the animal is having difficulty with the passage of urine or feces. If blood is present in the urine, notice whether it is passed at the beginning or the end of urination, or whether it is distributed throughout the entire passage of urine.

If blood is present in the feces, note its character. For example, is it bright red, or dark and tarry, what's the amount? Occasionally, entire specimens of internal parasites may be noticed in the feces. These should be collected in containers with tight fitting lids and promptly submitted to a veterinarian.

Temperature

Body temperature can readily be determined and is one of the best indications of the animal's state of health. The normal rectal temperature is between 101 and 102 F. Variations from this range frequently indicate an illness of some type. However, some variation in temperature may not be abnormal as—for example—a temperature rise following exercise or agitation.

A dog's temperature is always taken rectally; the thermometer is left in the rectum from 2 to 3 minutes before the reading is taken. Hold on to the thermometer to prevent it from completely entering the rectum. Lubrication of the thermometer with soap or mineral oil greatly increases the ease of its insertion. As a safety precaution, muzzle the dog before taking its temperature.

Kennel and adjacent area

In routine inspections always include a check of the inside of the kennel and the areas around it. If you keep your dog in the yard, walk around it and inspect it. This check may reveal evidence of vomiting, abnormal feces, or blood from a wound that might otherwise go unnoticed.

First Aid

The preceding chapter stressed the importance of reporting signs and symptoms of injury and disease to the veterinarian as soon as possible. However, there are times when the handler must take emergency measures to protect the health of his dog.

First aid is used in an emergency situation to save life, to prevent further injury, and to reduce pain. You should understand how and when first aid is used so that you may act in the best interests of the dog. In all emergency situations, notify the veterinarian as soon as possible, and seek and use the assistance of anyone who may be available.

Restraint

When a dog has been injured or is suffering from any condition in which it experiences acute pain or distress, urgent action is required. In this case, the animal may respond to its handler's attention in an unpredictable manner.

The dog may struggle violently and even attempt to bite. These are natural and normal reactions for a dog under such circumstances, but these reactions may result in further injury to the dog, to the handler, or to anyone assisting the handler.

It is important that you properly control and restrain your dog before attempting to administer first aid in any emergency situation. You should approach the distressed animal in the correct manner. Because of the close relationship you have with your dog, you should be able to approach it with confidence; the animal knows and trusts you. As you confidently get close to it, speak in a soothing and calm voice. In this way you can overcome the dog's fear or apprehension.

Whether or not to apply a muzzle depends on the nature of the situation. If the animal is unconscious, a leather muzzle must not be applied. If there is difficulty in breathing or if there are severe wounds about the head, it is not wise to use a muzzle. In most cases, however, a muzzle should be used to protect yourself or anyone helping you.

There are several types of muzzles which may be used, and the regular leather basket muzzle is the best of these. This is the most comfortable; it also permits freer breathing. It will cause the least alarm and apprehension since the dog is already familiar with it. The leather basket muzzle should be used whenever possible in an emergency situation. Remember, however, that the dog can still inflict a wound with such a muzzle on, so exercise caution.

Another type of muzzle which can be used is called the hasty muzzle. The actual application of this muzzle is a simple matter. First, tighten the choke chain on the dog's neck by pulling the leash tightly with the right hand. Place the left hand, palm up, under the choke chain on the dog's neck; grasp the leash tightly as it passes through the palm of the left hand. Then wrap the leash once around the dog's neck and bring it down the left side of the dog's head. Finally, wrap the leash twice around the dog's muzzle, and grasp it tightly with the left hand.

This type of muzzle may be used when the leather muzzle is not available or when it is believed that the leather muzzle would not provide adequate safety. Do not use the hasty muzzle when the dog is having difficulty in breathing or when there is an indication that it may vomit; do not leave it on for long periods of time in hot weather.

Still another type of muzzle which can be used is a makeshift muzzle constructed from a necktie, shoelace, piece of gauze bandage, or some other article. The easiest and most effective means of applying a makeshift muzzle is to place the center of a gauze strip under the dog's lower jaw and bring the ends up to tie a single knot about halfway between the nose and eyes. Bring the loose ends down one on each side of the mouth and cross them under the lower jaw. Bring the loose ends up behind the ears, one on each side of the neck, and tie them in a bowknot at the back of the head.

This type of muzzle has the same uses and the same limitations as the leash muzzle. Observe the dog closely and if it shows any difficulty in breathing or any indications that it may vomit, quickly remove it.

Wounds

A frequent emergency that arises with security dogs is the foot or leg wound in which there is active bleeding. In all bleeding wounds, the flow of blood (hemorrhage) must be controlled; this is the first thing to be done.

The quickest way to control bleeding of the foot or leg is to grasp the leg above the wound with the hand. Apply just enough pressure to control the bleeding. Replace the hand pressure with a tourniquet or pressure bandage as soon as possible. A tourniquet can be improvised from a number of articles, such as a leash, belt, necktie, shoelace, or a strip of cloth. A stick or similar object can be used to apply pressure.

Remember that the tourniquet will interfere with the blood supply to the part of the leg below it; this can seriously damage the leg. Therefore, apply a tourniquet 3 or 4 inches above the wound with just enough pressure to control the bleeding. In case of a foot pad wound, a pressure bandage works better than a tourniquet.

Apply a pressure bandage as soon as possible to a leg or foot wound in which bleeding is a problem. Strips of cloth, gauze, bandaging material, and adhesive tape are useful in the construction of such a bandage.

Before applying these wrapping materials, place a clean piece of cloth or gauze immediately over the wound. Do not wrap the bandage tight enough to cut off circulation. It should be just tight enough to control the bleeding. Once the pressure bandage is securely in place, remove the tourniquet.

Never apply a bandage over a tourniquet because the tourniquet may be forgotten and left on too long. Remember, tourniquets are temporary devices and are to be used for the shortest possible periods of time. Seek veterinary service as soon as possible.

If bleeding occurs from a wound in an area where it is impossible to use a tourniquet, other means of controlling the hemorrhage must be taken. It may be possible to close the wound with your fingers, thus stopping the flow of blood. You may be able to stop the bleeding by making and applying a compress. To do this, press a piece of sterile dressing or a handkerchief over the wound and, if possible, secure the compress with a bandage. As in all cases of bleeding, do what you can to control it and then send or call for help.

Normally, the treatment of wounds is left to the veterinarian. Where necessary, however, certain things can be done in the preliminary treatment of skin wounds in which the urgent arrest of bleeding is not a problem. Trim the hair from the wound and wound edges, being careful that no hair falls into the wound; a moist, sterile gauze pad placed gently over the wound will prevent this. Flush the wound out thoroughly with water, and place a piece of clean, sterile gauze bandage over it for protection against further contamination.

Injuries

As described here, an injury occurs when the bones or internal organs of a dog have been damaged as a result of a blow, fall, a gunshot, or from some other cause.

Broken bones or fractures have not occurred with great frequency among guard dogs; however, injuries of this type do happen occasionally. Such injuries may occur when dogs are being transported from one place to another, or they may occur during training exercises at the confidence course. Most fractures that occur are in one or more of a dog's limbs. Regardless of how they happen, fractures are serious injuries.

If you know or suspect that a fracture has occurred, immediately restrain the animal properly so as to prevent possible injury to yourself. Make every effort to quiet the animal to minimize the possibility of further injury to the fracture site. Send for help; in the meantime keep the dog quiet and warm. The dog must be kept warm because some degree of shock usually accompanies a serious fracture. Whenever possible, keep the dog at the place of injury until the veterinarian arrives. If this is not practical because of weather conditions or the time factor, move the dog.

Before moving a dog with a fractured leg, it is advisable to apply a splint to the leg whenever possible. You cannot splint those leg fractures that occur high on the limb. Splinting consists of fastening the leg to a firm object such as a stick or board by means of adhesive tape, gauze bandage, strips of cloth, the leash or other suitable material.

The splint is designed to immobilize the leg at the fracture site and to prevent further injury. Apply the splint firmly but not so tightly that blood circulation in the leg is impaired. If the ends of the broken bone are protruding through the skin, cover the area with a clean, sterile gauze bandage before applying the splint.

Splinting must be done before attempting to transport the dog. A litter can be made from available materials. Care must be exercised to prevent the dog from jumping off the litter and sustaining further injury.

Do NOT attempt to set the fracture. This causes the dog to suffer needlessly and might result in greater damage at the fracture site. This is a job that must be done by a veterinarian.

Injury to internal organs of the body may be accompanied by internal bleeding and shock, in which case paleness of the membranes of the dog's mouth and eyes, or difficulty in breathing, may be apparent. Sometimes, the inner surface of the lips feel cold. If you suspect that your dog may be suffering from internal injuries, keep it as warm and quiet as possible. Seek assistance immediately; and if it is necessary to move the animal, use a litter to carefully transport it.

It is not desirable to overwarm an animal in shock. It is better that it be slightly cool than too warm. The prevention of heat loss from under the dog is equally as important as covering. Just enough covering to prevent excess loss of body heat is needed.

Do not offer water to an injured dog. Its tongue may be moistened, but the drinking of water is prohibited when internal injuries are suspected.

Snakebites

In the event a dog is bitten by a poisonous snake, and after the snake is killed and saved for identification, try to keep the dog quiet and calm. Send for help immediately. The dog must be transported to a treatment facility in a vehicle or carried in the handler's arms. Poison moves more rapidly through the bloodstream when panic or exertion occurs; therefore, it is emphasized that the dog be kept as quiet as possible.

Bites mainly occur on the face or neck; in these cases, immediately remove the choke chain and be prepared to loosen or remove the collar (and/or muzzle). Swelling occurs rapidly after a snakebite, and these items of equipment may interfere with breathing. It is extremely important that the veterinarian be notified as quickly as possible. When possible, bring the dead snake with the dog to the veterinarian; this is an invaluable aid in determining what course of treatment to start.

Foreign objects in the mouth

A dog may occasionally get a stick or some other foreign object lodged in its mouth or throat. When this occurs, the animal may cough and gag, have difficulty in swallowing, paw at the mouth, and drool. Should these symptoms appear, be very cautious because an animal with rabies may show similar symptoms. If the dog is obviously having great difficulty in breathing and you can see the foreign object, attempt to remove it.

Poisoning

You can usually prevent your dog from becoming poisoned. In the approach to all types of diseases and injuries, prevention is the desired goal. With the dog under careful control, it is not a great problem to prevent it from eating anything except its normal ration. If food material other than that in its ration is discovered in a place where the dog can find it, it must be regarded with suspicion. Don't permit your dog to eat it.

Such a discovery might suggest the possibility of an attempt by an intruder to perform some act of sabotage. A possible source of poisoning for dogs is rat poison. There are several types of rat poison, and many of them are harmful to dogs. Such agents are used in the kennel area only by a professional insect and rodent agency and with the approval of the veterinarian.

The signs of poisoning vary with the poison concerned and may be similar to those of many disease conditions. Unless you are certain your dog has eaten a poisonous substance, it is not wise to treat it for poisoning. If, in spite of all precautions, the animal has eaten poison, immediate action is necessary.

If a veterinarian is not immediately available, give the dog something to cause vomiting; a salt solution can safely be used for this purpose. Such a solution can be prepared by adding a tablespoonful of salt to a glass of water. Give the salt solution by mouth, in the same manner as liquid medicine, until vomiting occurs. Keep the dog quiet and warm until a veterinarian is able to see it.

Heat stroke

Heat stroke represents a very serious medical emergency in which immediate action may be necessary to save the animal's life. Heat stroke results when a dog is unable to eliminate its body heat rapidly enough. In the summertime, or in hot climates, overheating is seen occasionally in working dogs; overheating may even occur at night. In hot weather, a dog may become overheated during training and when it is being transported. Symptoms of heat stroke may include weakness, unsteady gait, vomiting, difficult or labored breathing, convulsions, and collapse; there is a very high body temperature of 106°-107° or more.

First aid treatment consists of carrying the animal as rapidly as possible to the nearest shade and quickly lowering the body heat of the animal. Body heat can be lowered by pouring water on the animal's head, body, and stomach, and fanning this same area with a shirt or anything else available. If a stream or body of water is available, immerse the animal; be sure that its head is above water at all times so that water cannot get into the lungs. If ice is available, massage it over the body and legs. Ice packs may be placed on the inside of the forelegs near the body or on the inside of the dog's thighs. Large blood vessels are close to the surface in these areas and body temperature can be rapidly lowered by this means.

If the animal must be moved more than a few yards to the shade or to the treatment facility, hand carry or transport it in a vehicle. Walking or running it only serves to increase the overheating problem. To prevent overheating, keep training and vigorous exercise to a minimum in very hot weather; allow frequent rest periods and provide small amounts of drinking water at frequent intervals. Also, adequate ventilation is necessary when a dog is being transported.

Feeding

To keep your dog in a state of good health a proper diet is necessary. Such a diet must satisfy the energy requirements of the animal, and provide all the essential components of a balanced ration.

In this section, consideration will be given to what a good diet must contain and also what, when, and how much to feed.

A dog's diet requires basically the same essential components as does that of a human. It must contain sufficient quantities of protein, carbohydrates, fats, vitamins, and minerals. A dog also requires a certain amount of water each day.

Proteins are sometimes called tissue builders. This means that they are primarily involved in the growth and structure of the tissues of the body (muscles, tendons). Fats and carbohydrates are more commonly referred to as energy producers, that is, they provide the necessary fuel so that the body is able to work.

Vitamins (A, B1, D) and minerals (calcium, iron, phosphorus) serve a wide variety of uses in a dog's body. Calcium, phosphorus and vitamin D, for example, are involved in bone structure and growth. Vitamin A plays an important role in vision, iron is an important component of the blood.

Some of the dog foods which are high in proteins are horse meat, beef, liver meal, fish meal, milk and eggs. Carbohydrates are found in large amounts in sugars, starches, and cellulose which are contained in such foods as corn, potatoes, oats, barley, rice, wheat, and candy. Butter, lard, and vegetable oils are examples of foods which are high in fat content.

Vitamins and minerals are found in a wide variety of foods. For example, milk and bone meal are high in calcium content, cod liver oil in vitamin D and A, meat and oatmeal in vitamin B1.

Water is a component of the food which you feed your dog. But there is not enough water in the food to supply all of the animal's needs. A continuous supply of fresh, clean water in adequate quantities must always be available.

What to feed

A high quality commercially prepared dog food should be used to insure that your dog is getting the required amounts of protein, carbohydrates, fats, vitamins and minerals. Compared to the old feeding method of using homemade mixtures of meats and vegetables, the use of commercially prepared food conserves time, labor and storage space.

Most important, the commercial dog food made to guaranteed analysis, and in accordance with national standards insures that the animal is receiving a scientifically balanced, nutritionally adequate diet.

How much to feed

Once a good commercial dog food has been found, the problem of how much to feed the animal must be considered. This problem is largely one of determining the energy requirements of the dog. A calorie is a unit of heat, and is the term used to express the fuel or energy value of food. A dog must obtain a certain amount of energy from its food each day; therefore each dog has certain caloric requirements.

It has been determined that the adult defensive dog requires about 35 to 50 calories daily per pound of body weight. To obtain caloric balance it should eat 1 pound of dry-type dog food per 40 pounds of body weight, or 1 pound of soft-moist food per 34 pounds of body weight; 1 pound of canned dog food per 14 pounds of body weight, or 1 pound of high-calorie diet per 64 pounds of body weight.

Working dogs would require 50 calories per pound of body weight which would be met by the following amounts of food daily: dry-type, 1 pound per 27 pounds of body weight. Soft-moist, 1 pound per 24 pounds of body weight. Canned food, 1 pound per 10 pounds of body weight, and high-calorie diet, 1 pound per 45 pounds of body weight. These figures are given in the table below.

TYPE OF RATION	AT REST	AT WORK
Dry	1-lb/40-lbs	1-lb/27-lbs
Soft-moist	1-lb/34-lbs	1-lb/24-lbs
Canned	1-lb/14-lbs	1-lb/10-lbs
High-calorie	1-lb/64-lbs	1-lb/45-lbs

The feeding of a security dog is not quite as simple as it may appear. There is more involved than mere computation of figures. Not all dogs of the same body weight require exactly the same amount of food.

Several factors are responsible for this; one of these is the type of climate in which a dog is living. The calories and food requirements for dogs working in hot climates are less than for cold climates.

Another factor is the temperature of the animal. If the dog is high strung and nervous, and if it constantly runs and paces in the kennel or yard, then it has a greater calorie requirement than a more placid animal.

Another factor involves the conditions under which the animal must work. If it is working long hours of course its caloric requirements will be greater. Food utilization is also a factor. Some dogs can digest and utilize their food better than others and hence can eat less to get the same amount of available energy.

Finally, there's the health factor. If a dog is not in good health, it might require more or less calories than when healthy, depending on the type of illness.

The existence of these variable factors leads to the conclusion that, although the estimated average calorie and food requirements for security dogs have been established by the military and professional breeders, feeding is still an individual matter. Each dog should receive the amount of food needed to maintain proper weight and physical condition.

How and when to feed

There are two feeding methods presently used. The pan feeding method is the basic method, and involves feeding the dog once a day from the feeding pan. Allow the food to remain in the kennel area for a period of time, usually ½ hour. Remove the pan after that time, discard the remaining food, and clean the pan. Dry dog food may be fed as is or mixed with water.

The food-reward method involves variations of the basic method just described with incorporation of a food reward technique used in training.

You can determine how much food your dog receives daily by observation of the animal's average food intake requirements and by consideration of the variable factors which affect these requirements.

With the pan-feeding method, when to feed is important. It depends largely on the training or work schedule of the dog. Avoid feeding just before or after strenuous exercise. Violent exercise after a heavy meal pre-disposes a dog to gastric torsion (twisting of the stomach or "flip-flop" stomach) bloat, or some other gastrointestinal illness. Don't feed your dog just after it has come in from a training period because this interferes with digestion.

Behavior and Motivation

The behavior of the security dog is the result of many factors. Some of these are heredity, natural instincts, basic senses, past experiences, and basic drives. Because of the depth and complexity of this subject, only those behavioral factors which are most important in the training and utilization of protection dogs are considered here.

In this section, special emphasis is given to a dog's basic senses. Not only must the factors influencing behavior be recognized but also the types of behavior dogs exhibit must be considered. The behavior exhibited by dogs can be discussed using many of the same terms used in referring to human behavior. The behavioral characteristics considered essential in training security dogs are sensitivity, energy, aggressiveness, intelligence, and willingness.

Basic senses

Dogs and humans possess the same basic senses. Both use their senses to detect and alert on persons or objects which are foreign to a given area. The senses of a dog, in order of importance to training are smell, hearing, sight, and touch.

Smell

One of the main reasons why dogs have been selected for protection work is that they have a keen sense of smell. Studies have shown that a dog responds to odor traces of all known sorts and dilutions far more extreme than can be detected by man. Furthermore, dogs can distinguish between many odors which seem to human beings to be similar. The dog's sense of smell is invaluable because a great part of its role as a detector depends on its ability to pick up a scent.

Hearing

The dog's sense of hearing is another reason why this animal is invaluable when used in security operations. A dog has an acute sense of hearing; it can detect sound twenty times better than a man; which means that it can detect sounds that would completely escape notice of a person.

Its sense of hearing is also important because it is the principal medium through which you communicate with it. Some dogs appear to understand accurately the feelings and wishes of their owners as they are conveyed by voice. Usually a word spoken in an encouraging tone, such as "good boy", pleases a dog. A cross word such as the admonition "no", tends to depress the animal.

It is important that your dog respond to a number of oral commands, for it soon learns to associate the sound and tone of a word with the action expected of it.

Sight

Besides being taught to react correctly to voice commands, the dog must also be taught to obey hand gestures. It does this through its sense of sight. With one exception—the ability to detect movement—a dog's vision cannot be compared favorably with that of the human. To the dog, everything probably appears to be constantly blurred and out of focus. In addition, it is probably unable to discriminate between colors, and sees everything as a black and white or grayish picture.

It is not known at this time just how well a dog can see, or determine, colors. However, it can detect and respond to a moving object ten times better than a person.

Touch

There is a wide variation among dogs in their responsiveness to the sense of touch. Certain animals are very susceptible to caress or physical correction; others appear to be rather insensitive to it. Consequently, a dog's sense of touch can be determined when it is petted or corrected. Some dogs seem to understand praise or correction better physically than orally.

Sensitivity

The term "sensitivity" refers to the type and degree of response a dog shows to a certain stimulus. The oversensitive animal may be startled by a stimulus that would evoke only a mild response from an unsensitive dog. The response of the oversensitive animal is often one of shyness or fright. The unsensitive dog responding to the same stimulus might merely turn its head or show no response at all.

Sensitivity of sound and touch are completely independent of one another. For this reason, the sound of a gun may actually hurt a dog's ears and yet a slap with the hand may not bother it.

In selecting a dog, your characteristics should be matched with the sensitivity of the animal. Certain persons lack the proper range or tone of voice and are unable to appeal to a dog successfully through its hearing. However, these same persons may be excellent in handling a dog manually because of a certain fitness in muscular control and coordination.

There should be no difficulty in rating a dog's response to stimuli, and, from a practical standpoint, this rating becomes helpful. You can form a definite opinion about the response your dog shows toward the stimuli of sound and touch during normal day-to-day contact.

Oversensitive dogs

If a dog reacts excessively to a given stimulus, it may be oversensitive. An oversensitive dog is so handicapped that it is not likely to demonstrate its intelligence in a usable form.

Any dog which is oversensitive to either sound or touch, or both, is difficult to train and is usually considered unreliable. A dog that is oversensitive to sound may bolt at the sound of a gunshot. A dog that is oversensitive to touch may lie down and shake all over, as if frightened, when it is petted.

Unsensitive dogs

Dogs that are unsensitive to both sound and touch are difficult to train. A dog that is unsensitive to sound may not react at all when the stern admonition "no" is used. If it is unsensitive to touch, it may not react at all when you pet it. A dog unsensitive to either sound or touch, but not to both, can be instructed readily enough if the correct approach is used. In such a case, use either your voice or hand, whichever is appropriate.

Moderately sensitive dogs

A moderately sensitive dog is somewhat sensitive to both sound and touch. With proper training, this animal responds willingly to hand gestures and vocal commands. It is trustworthy, willing and ready to obey given commands.

The wisdom with which this dog is handled is the deciding factor in how well it performs. Properly trained, this dog is ideal for protection work.

Energy

Dogs differ not only in their degree of sensitivity but also in the degree of energy they show. A dog's behavior with regard to energy is quite evident. The term "energy" as used here refers to the degree of spontaneous activity of the animal—the speed and extent of its movements in general—not in response to any particular command.

Dogs differ widely in the degree of spontaneous activity exhibited, and the task of rating them in this respect is easier than that of rating for other functional traits. Different dogs show two extreme degrees of energy—one dog is the shiftless, lazy animal, which shows no energy whatever unless required. The other is the animal that seems eager to move, wants to be active, and seems to be always on the go.

The average dog is between these two extremes, a willing worker but not always on the go. Above average energy is not particularly necessary for security purposes, but a dog that possesses this trait can be trained to control some of its extra energy. An animal that shows little or no energy is difficult to train and should be avoided.

Aggressiveness

A dog that's energetic is not necessarily aggressive. There are three general degrees: overaggressive, unaggressive, and moderately aggressive. Each dog should be classified for aggressiveness to determine what action is necessary to decrease its aggressiveness, increase it, or perhaps maintain it at a constant level.

Overaggressive dog

When an overaggressive dog sights a decoy, it usually becomes greatly excited, lunges at the end of its leash, and continues to lunge after the decoy disappears. Caution must be exercised while working with an overaggressive animal because it may attempt to bite anyone within reach during a period of excitement. Training procedures are designed to control, rather than arouse, the overaggressive dog.

Unaggressive dog

This type of animal reacts negatively to the approach of a decoy. It may stand still, wag its tail, throw itself on the ground, or try to run away from the decoy. Training procedures consist of exercises which tend to develop confidence and courage in the unaggressive dog.

Moderately aggressive dog

The ideal defensive dog is moderately aggressive. This type of animal is the easiest to train. Upon seeing a decoy it becomes alert, shows suspicion of the decoy, and exhibits an eagerness to move towards it.

The majority of German Shepherd dogs fall into the moderately aggressive category, and normal training procedures are based upon this type of aggressiveness.

Intelligence

Generally, intelligence is the trait most closely related to a dog's success in training for protection work. Among the lower animals, the dog is rated as highly intelligent. It can be taught to respond correctly to a large number of spoken words. Only a few words are needed under ordinary conditions, but some dogs have been known to respond to over 100 oral commands.

A dog's rating for intelligence is based upon its ability to retain and use what it has learned. It can be rated high in intelligence if it is unusually capable of profiting by experience. A highly intelligent dog may be successful only when working with a handler who pleases it. With another handler, it may be unwilling and give the appearance of being stupid.

Willingness

This term is an arbitrary one used to refer to the dog's reaction to the commands given. It applies to the way it responds to a command and its apparent cheerfulness and acceptance in learning new duties. The dog may make the correct response to a command, or it may make some other response. In either case, if it makes an enthusiastic attempt, it is considered willing.

A dog is ranked high in willingness if it continuously responds to a given command in an effort to fulfill it, even though reward or correction is not immediate. Whether the animal possesses the required intelligence and physical strength, or whether it succeeds or fails, is not considered in determining willingness.

If you must constantly coax your dog along or admonish it before it works satisfactorily, it is considered an unwilling worker. A great number of dogs are perfectly capable of executing the required movements but are strongly inclined not to do so.

An unwilling dog may appear to make a distinction between work and play, and may take great pleasure in retrieving, searching for objects, and in taking jumps. The same animal may at times come to you spontaneously and apparently suggest a romp which may include any of the mentioned acts. When this situation is reversed and you initiate the activity, the dog, if unwilling, may seem to have forgotten all it knew.

You can advance or retard your dog's willingness. Improper handling may make it less willing at one time than another time. For example, if you lack patience, the dog may work willingly during the first few minutes of a training period, but unwillingly during the remainder of the period.

Unwillingness can be confused with a lack of intelligence or with lack of sensitivity. If the correct approach is not used, a dog that is unsensitive to either sound or touch may appear to behave unwillingly to the commands and motivation given by the handler.

Motivation

As you become familiar with your dog's behavior, you should learn the correct approach to use to motivate it. Dogs should always be motivated with an intangible reward.

Intangible reward

Unlike most animals, dogs don't require special inducements, such as food, to work or train. Kindness, shown either by oral praise or by casual caress, is usually enough to thoroughly motivate these animals. More than any other form of reward, it wants the approval of its handler.

A dog seems to have a natural tendency to become attached to and to seek companionship from its handler. The handler feeds, grooms, trains and works it. As a result of this, the animal responds to commands, reacts to correction, and accepts praise. Through the constant use of the oral admonition "no" when it misbehaves or otherwise needs correcting, the dog learns to distinguish between praise and correction.

The dog is eager to please you, and if it is praised each time it does its work correctly, it is anxious to advance to new training exercises. It is important that you honor its affection.

After a friendly relationship has been established between you and your dog, this relationship becomes the motivation needed to train the animal to become an efficient worker.

Some type of corrective action must always be present; yet it is more pleasant and more convenient to rely upon the dog's willingness to serve you. A security dog is properly trained only when motivated by an intangible rather than a tangible reward.

Training Equipment

The proper choice and use of equipment is important because the security dog learns to associate each item of equipment with some activity in which it is involved.

Through proper use of these items, you can communicate your wishes to the animal and control and discipline it. Each piece of equipment has been designed for a specific purpose. You should become acquainted with what the items are and how and why they are used in a certain way.

The items of equipment described in this section are recommended because they have been tested and proved satisfactory for training purposes. This by no means implies that changes and improvements to equipment cannot be made to meet your special requirements.

Leather collar

The dog wears a leather collar while it is —
1) chained to a stake
2) secured to a kennel
3) being transported

When putting the leather collar on, tighten it enough to insert only two fingers between the collar and the dog's neck. This is done to prevent the collar from slipping off and to make sure that it is not too loose.

After the collar is adjusted and buckled in place, run the end of the collar through the loop so the buckle will not come unfastened.

Choke chain

Another item the dog wears around its neck is the choke chain. This item is normally worn during obedience training, while being taken to and from the kennel, or while being transported in a vehicle.

The choke chain must be worn correctly. Instructions for putting on the choke chain are as follows:
1) Hold one of the rings of the chain in the right hand between the thumb and index finger. Hold the other ring in your left hand between the thumb and index finger. Hold the ring in the left hand so that it is in a flat or horizontal position.
2) Raise the right hand directly over the left hand. Allow the lengths of chain between the two rings to fall through the ring held in the left hand.
3) Place the choke chain over the dog's head.
4) Snap the leash into the ring on the free end of the choke chain.

When the choke chain is on correctly, the pull of the leash is from left to right when the dog is on your left or "heel" side. This permits the chain to release when slack is given in

Correctly placed choke chain.

the leash. If pull is from right to left, the chain clings to the dog's neck and continues to choke it even though the leash has slack.

Training leash

Two training leashes are used in dog work.

Leather, 60-inch

The 60-inch leather leash is used during training. When necessary, the leather leash can be secured to your wrist; this is known as a safety leash. To do this:
1) Thread the snap end of the leash through the loop end, forming a loop which can be loosened or tightened.
2) Insert right hand into the newly formed loop.
3) Pull the snap end of the leash away from the loop end and tighten the leash around wrist.

Nylon-web, 300-inch

The 300-inch leash is always used in intermediate obedience training to control the animal. When necessary, you can secure the 300-inch leash to your right wrist in the same manner as the 60-inch leash.

Kennel chain

The 6-foot kennel chain is used for tying the dog to stationary objects. This chain should always be used with the leather collar and should never be tied directly to the dog's neck.

Muzzle

A muzzle is a device by which you can prevent your dog from injuring other dogs, innocent people, or itself. Normally a dog doesn't wear a muzzle during training periods because it is distracting and the animal devotes its efforts towards removing it. Thus, the benefits of training are lost.

Dogs that are known to be aggressive should be muzzled while being groomed. Although grooming is generally enjoyable for the animal, it does not preclude its biting. Any muzzle, particularly if it is too large or incorrectly adjusted, is not a guarantee against being bitten.

To put the muzzle on the dog:
1) Hold the basket of the muzzle in your right hand. Fold all straps back over the basket of the muzzle.
2) Place the basket of the muzzle over the dog's nose and mouth. Bring the straps back over its head.
3) Secure the straps.

Be certain the muzzle you have selected is fitted to your animal. The side straps must be adjusted so the dog's nose is not jammed against the inside of the basket.

The strap around the neck must be fastened tight enough to keep the muzzle on properly and yet afford proper breathing. Check the fit of the muzzle from time to time because the straps stretch with age.

Comb

There are several types of grooming combs. Pick a quality one at any pet shop.

When combing your dog, comb lightly with the grain, never against it. Always exert enough pressure on the comb to remove loose hair and all foreign matter, such as mud, from the coat.

Use the comb sparingly since excessive combing removes the undercoat and may scratch or cut the skin.

Brush

Grooming brushes vary in size and shape. These are also available in pet shops. The ideal brush is approximately the size of a man's hand and has firm, stiff bristles.

Feeding pan

The feeding pan should have at least a 3-quart capacity. This is large enough to hold the dog's daily ration and allows it enough room to eat.

A heavy gauge, stainless steel pan is recommended. This type of pan is easy to keep clean and serviceable. Wash and sanitize the feeding pan immediately after each feeding.

Water bucket

Another essential item of equipment is the water bucket. It should be either steel or heavy gauge galvanized iron, and have at least a 3½-gallon capacity. Clean the bucket daily, as fresh water should always be available to the dog.

Principles of Dog Training

Know-how

The most fundamental principle of training is that you must know how each maneuver, act, technique, method, and position is accomplished before you can properly train your dog.

There are standards of performance described for each training exercise. You must adhere to the proper methods and techniques so that these standards are achieved. You must conscientiously apply all of the principles with interest, enthusiasm, and a desire to attain perfection. You must demand complete obedience from your dog at all times.

If you become negligent in your training procedures, the

results will be reflected in the dog's performance. It is essential that you possess personal discipline. This is especially true during the time you are applying the principle of repetition.

Repetition

The method by which dogs learn and become proficient in performing a task is repetition. It is essential that the dog be given the same command over and over again until the desired response is obtained. However, both you and your dog can lose efficiency by practicing any one command too many times during one period. After practicing a command for 4 or 5 minutes, it is best to move to another command. If this is not possible, at least 10 minutes should elapse before resuming practice of the original command.

In the early stages of training, it's important to show the dog what to do when given a particular command. If necessary, the dog must be put into the proper position. Repeat the procedure as often as necessary until the animal learns what to do when given the command. Never allow the dog to assume a position incorrectly. If it begins to make an incorrect movement, correct it immediately; then, begin the exercise again, making sure that it doesn't make the same mistake.

Patience

One of the most important requirements you will need in order to correctly train your dog is patience. To make a dog perform the same exercise repeatedly until it is properly executed is a task that requires the ultimate in self-control. When you lose your temper, you lose control; this confuses the animal. Patience along with firmness results in a better trained dog.

Praise

The handler who displays patience can motivate his dog properly through praise. Whenever the dog successfully executes a command, even if its performance has taken more time than expected, always reward it with a pat on the head or praise it in some other way. It is anxious to please you, and you should respond by praising it lavishly. When it is praised highly, the dog senses that it has done the correct thing, and does it more readily the next time the same command is given.

Several effective methods are used to praise a dog. Kind words often do the trick. One person might prefer to pat his dog each time he wishes to reward it. Another might allow his dog a few minutes in which to romp and play, or he may allow the animal to perform its favorite exercises. Still another handler may apply a combination of these methods. Each dog requires a special method. Each person must determine which method of praise best suits his dog. This can be done during the owner's early association with the animal.

If you are to maintain your animal's enthusiasm for work, each training period must be concluded with petting, praise, and encouragement. When the performance of the training exercise does not warrant praise, allow it to perform a short exercise which it knows thoroughly and does well so that it can earn a reward. Although the dog must be amply rewarded for those exercises performed correctly, it must be corrected when its performance is not satisfactory.

Correction

A dog does not understand right from wrong as humans do. Reward and correction are the means by which it is taught. If the animal does an exercise incorrectly, do not allow it to go uncorrected. Withholding praise, or the simple admonition "no", spoken reprovingly, or a sharp jerk on the leash, usually proves to be sufficient for correction purposes.

Timing is probably the most important factor in administering any form of correction. A reprimand, in whatever form, should be administered immediately when the incorrect act is performed. Dogs cannot mentally connect a reprimand with an incorrect action committed sometime before.

Never correct a dog for clumsiness, slowness in learning, or inability to understand what is expected of it. In these cases, correction slows down the training instead of accelerating it.

Observation, patience, self-control, and discretion are essential in correction. If the dog makes a mistake, you may be at fault, and you should think for a second about why the mistake was made. Proper correction indicates proper thinking.

Obedience Training

Basic training

Obedience training produces a reliable, obedient, well-trained dog. The specific methods of training outlined in this chapter are suitable for the fundamental training of all defensive dogs. In certain cases where the prescribed method may prove ineffective, the trainer may vary his techniques to achieve the desired level of training.

The normal training period consists of approximately 20 minutes of obedience training followed by a 10 minute break. However, the age of the dog, climatic conditions, and the overall conditioning of the animal may govern the length of the training period. During break periods, it is important that the dog be given an opportunity to rest and relax. In hot climates, it should have a place to rest which provides some type of shade.

Basic obedience training is applicable to both man and dog. You must first learn the different movements before you can begin training the dog. Then, you must teach the animal the different movements and commands.

Most commands are one syllable words, and they are easily given. If the commands are given clearly, they are easy for the dog to learn. Even though a word may have no meaning to a dog, it learns to associate the sound of a word with the exercise it is to perform.

Formations

Three types of formations are used to teach the dog basic obedience. Each formation is designed for a specific purpose, however, each is flexible enough to be used for other training purposes. Basic obedience usually begins in the circle formation.

Circle

The HEEL position is one of the first that the dog learns. It can learn this quite rapidly in a formation that requires the animal to walk to your left side without making any sharp turns. In the circle formation, the dog walks around in a circle at the handler's side. You can reverse your direction, or, when necessary, stop and stand facing either the inside or the outside of the imaginary circle.

Other commands can be taught in this type of formation, such as SIT, DOWN, and STAY.

Square

The square formation is used to teach movements which require sharp turns. Either left or right turns can be made from this formation, depending on the direction in which you are walking. This is an excellent formation to use in teaching the dog to stay in the correct heel position when making a sharp turn. Keep the animal close to your sides as you execute turns.

Line

The line formation can be used effectively to teach commands which require you and the dog to be separated by the length of the leash. This formation is especially helpful when teaching the commands of STAY and COME.

The line formation is also used for intermediate and advanced obedience training when a dog is learning to react to commands given from a greater distance than the length of the leather leash. This formation is also used during agitation training.

Commands

While training your dog, use both your voice and hands to convey commands to the animal. If it is to react favorably to commands, you must have its undivided attention. Not only must you know what responses are expected from the dog, but you must also know how to achieve the desired responses. You can then proceed with confidence in yourself and your ability to use the commands properly.

Use of commands

Simple commands are used to teach obedience. They are short words or signals which, when given properly, are easy for a dog to grasp. You will use both oral commands and hand gestures in training. Therefore, it is of the utmost importance that you give these commands and gestures in a correct manner.

Oral

The word used in an oral command is of little importance.

It is the sound of the word that the dog associates with the movement required. For this reason, you must consistently give the command in the same manner and in the same tone of voice. It doesn't matter if your voice is high or low pitched; but you must always use the same firm, clear, decisive tone of voice in giving a command.

Hand gestures

Hand gestures are taught so that in actual working situations the dog will respond to silent commands. When first introduced they are given simultaneously with the appropriate oral command. Voice commands and hand gestures can be given independently after both you and your dog become proficient in the use of the commands. As training progresses, the animal learns what is expected of it when the appropriate gesture is given.

Commands taught

The commands taught during basic obedience training are used throughout your association with your dog. The proficiency gained in basic obedience is reflected in all further training and working of the animal.

Heel

The initial command in dog training is the command HEEL. All additional commands or exercises start and end in the heel position. The dog is trained to walk, stand, or sit at your left side, with its right shoulder in line with your left knee. Its body should be parallel with your body, and it must neither forge ahead nor lag behind.

The verbal command is HEEL, and the gesture command is made by slapping the left leg with the left hand open. During initial training, the verbal command and hand gesture are given simultaneously until the dog becomes proficient. These commands can be given individually or need not be given at all when the animal has learned to stay in the proper heel position.

Most verbal commands cannot be taught independently of each other. The commands SIT, STAY, and NO are taught in conjunction with the command HEEL. (Each of these commands is explained in detail later.)

During initial training, HEEL may be used frequently as a training aid, but after the dog has learned this command, it should not be used excessively. As the animal develops proficiency, give the command HEEL only when it starts, halts, or changes directions. For example:

1) When walking forward, the command HEEL is given simultaneously with the first forward step.
2) On movements toward the left or right, the command is given as you pivot.
3) When coming to a stop, the command HEEL is given one pace before halting.

When walking with you, the dog may get out of the heel position by moving ahead. Correct it by giving a sharp jerk on the leash and by repeating the command HEEL. When necessary, give the command NO just before repeating the command HEEL. When the dog lags behind, it is coaxed into the proper heal position, not jerked.

When you stop, your dog should assume the heel position. If it does not get in the proper position, it must be corrected immediately. When the dog is not facing in the right direction, place your left hand, palm up, lightly under its abdomen and shift it until it faces in the proper direction.

A dog that gets in a position that is too close to the handler can be corrected by placing the left hand against the right side of the animal's abdomen and pushing gently. When the dog is too far away, place your left hand on its left hip and pull it into proper position.

No

The command NO is a verbal reprimand and must be given in a harsh, firm voice. This command is used to correct the dog after it has made a mistake. At the command NO, the dog should cease that activity for which it is being corrected. If the command isn't enough to correct the animal, a jerk on the leash is used in conjunction with the command. This type of correction is used continually throughout training whenever the dog shows any lack of obedience to your commands.

Observe your dog closely at all times and give the command NO if it begins to break position or perform incorrectly. For example, if it is in the down position and decides to sit up, you can readily spot it preparing to move and can immediately give the command NO. By using this procedure, you can usually prevent your dog from making improper movements.

Sit

The command SIT is taught in conjunction with the command HEEL. In the heel-sit position, the dog sits beside your left leg. Its body is parallel to, and its right shoulder in line with, your left knee.

When given the command SIT, the dog may be either standing or lying down. Upon hearing the command, it must promptly assume a sitting position. After learning the command SIT, it must automatically sit without command when coming to a stop from walking.

The command SIT is given in a sharp, concise tone of voice. When this command is given, grasp the leash several inches above the choke chain with your right hand. Place your left hand over the hips of the animal with the fingers positioned on the base of the tail. Give an upward jerk on the leash and push down and forward on its croup with the left hand.

You must not place your left hand on the dog's back or too high on its hips. As training progresses and the dog learns what it is expected to do when given the command SIT, physical assistance is no longer required.

If the dog does not sit facing directly forward, swing its body around into the correct position. This is done by using the left hand to push or pull its hindquarters into the desired position. If it sits behind you or too far from your side, pull its head to the left side with the leash. The left hand is used to restrain the dog to prevent it from getting up and following the leash. This type of correction is most effective if given just as the animal is in the act of sitting, before its hindquarters have touched the ground.

During the introduction of the command SIT, the dog may get slightly out of position; if this happens, don't force it into the right position. After the animal learns what is expected of it and becomes more proficient, you can then make corrections on its positions. It must be praised each time it assumes the correct sitting position.

You may also give the command SIT while you are out in front of your dog at the end of the leash. In this position, the dog is in the standing position facing towards you.

During the introduction of SIT from the end of the leash, hold the end of the leash in your left hand. Step forward one step with your right foot, grasp the leash approximately 12 inches from the choke chain and give an upward jerk and the verbal command SIT.

After giving the gesture and verbal command STAY, bring your right foot back alongside your left foot. Once the dog becomes proficient in the command SIT, discontinue the step-in with the right foot; instead, give the proper hand gesture in addition to the verbal command.

To give this gesture, hold the end of the leash in your left hand and make an upward gesture with your right hand. If the dog continues to disobey, jerk it with the leash while at the same time giving the command SIT. Because the animal needs to be jerked and not pulled, you should hit or slap the leash instead of grabbing. This produces a quick jerk instead of a pulling sensation.

Stay

When the dog has shown obedience to the preceding commands, you may begin teaching the command STAY. This command is also given in a firm tone of voice. It may be given while the animal is in any position. On hearing the command STAY, the dog must stay in the same position which it held when given the command. Furthermore, it must remain in that position until you give it another command.

Initial training in the command STAY is conducted while the dog is in the sit position. When it is at your side, either standing, sitting, or lying down, the gesture for it to stay is given simultaneously with the oral command. To do this, give the command STAY in a firm, steady tone as you bring your left hand, palm towards the dog, back in a short, decisive gesture. Don't slap the animal but bring your hand straight back to its nose. This gesture conveys the necessary authority when skillfully executed; it appears as a threat when poorly executed.

To begin an exercise at the end of the leash, move from beside your dog to the end of the leash. To do this, the command STAY is given in a firm voice along with a decisive hand gesture; then, step forward with the right foot. The dog should not move when you take a step with your right foot. You should then walk to the end of the leash, turn around, and face the animal.

Don't move the full length of the leash away from the dog when this exercise is first practiced. Also to prevent the animal from becoming tired, the practice periods should be kept short. As the dog's performance improves, the distance between you and it are increased.

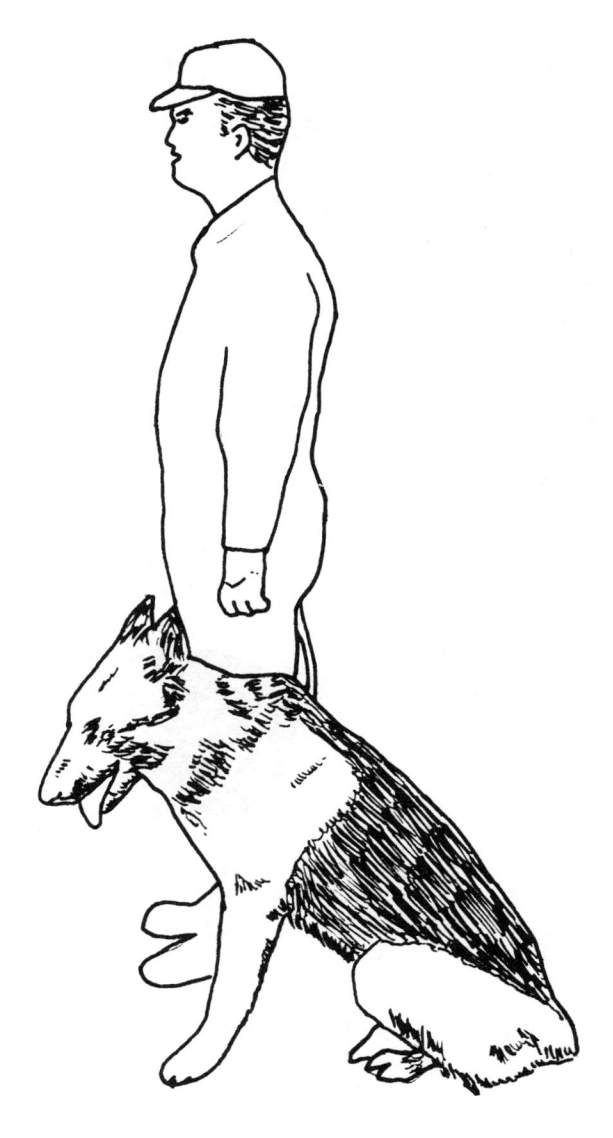

Sit position.

82   How to Train a Guard Dog

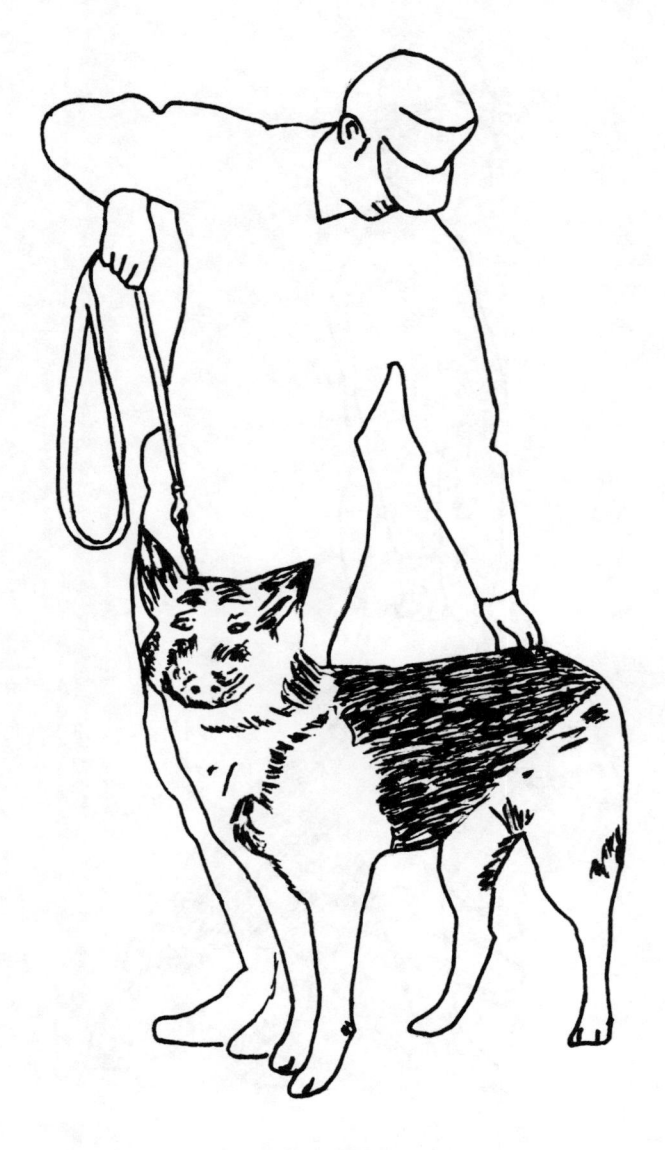

Teaching dog to sit.

How to Train a Guard Dog 83

Introducing dog to sit hand gesture at end of leash.

Sit hand gesture at end of leash.

While moving away from the animal to the end of the leash, change the leash from the right hand to the left; then, extend your arm and hand so that the palm of the hand faces directly towards the dog (like a traffic cop giving a stop signal). If the dog begins to move, correct it immediately. Give the command STAY. If the animal actually breaks position, give the commands NO, SIT (as the dog is put in the sit position), and STAY (as you give the proper hand gesture).

Down

As the dog's performance in executing the commands HEEL, SIT, NO, and STAY improves, start teaching it the command DOWN. Dogs frequently resist this exercise, therefore, it is not repeated too often in succession. To prevent this resistance, it sometimes helps if you alternate from this exercise to the heeling and sitting exercises.

In the down position, the dog lies parallel to your body, and its right shoulder is in line with your left foot. If the animal rolls on its side it is not in the down position and should be corrected immediately. Physical correction is made by placing the dog in the proper position and by giving the command STAY.

When given the command DOWN, the dog must lie down promptly. When you first introduce this command, it should be in the heel-sit position. The command is given in a firm, steady voice; at the same time, bend down and place your left hand on the leash just above the snap. As you give the verbal command DOWN, pull down on the leash with the left hand. (If the dog has a small neck, it may cause slack in the chain. In this case, it may be necessary to grab the choke chain instead of the leash to have enough room to pull downward.) If pulling on the leash does not put the dog in the down position, you will have to simultaneously pull its front legs forward.

After it is in the down position, the command STAY (in

Stay hand gesture, handler beside dog.

How to Train a Guard Dog 87

Stay hand gesture, handler in front of dog.

conjunction with the hand gesture for STAY) is given so that the dog remains in place without changing positions.

Use extreme caution during the introduction of the command DOWN, because the dog may resent the use of force. Your position is such that you could easily be bitten if the animal snapped. The left hand may be used as an effective aid to safety because it is on the choke chain, and you can push the dog away from your face, leg, or right hand.

After the dog has executed the DOWN command satisfactorily, it is kept in position for a short time while you stand at its right side. Then give it the command SIT, and if it comes to the sit position satisfactorily, praise it highly. If its performance is unsatisfactory, give the command SIT, and at the same time jerk up on the leash. This should cause the dog to sit up. If this fails, give the commands NO, SIT and jerk harder on the leash.

Repeat this exercise, using the command DOWN until the animal ceases to resist it. If at any time the dog shows signs that it may break position, correct it by using the command STAY. If it needs correction while it is in the down position, don't move your feet because this may confuse it. When the dog breaks position, immediately put it back in the sit position and again give the command DOWN.

As the dog's performance of the command DOWN improves, you should refrain from pulling down on the choke chain until it has an opportunity to obey the command and gesture.

When it becomes proficient at executing the command DOWN, you can begin another exercise using the same command. With the dog in the sit position, give the command STAY; you should then move to the end of the leash, changing the leash to your left hand before completing the move. Step forward one step with your right foot and grasp the leash about 6 inches from the choke chain. Give a downward jerk and the verbal command DOWN. Once the dog is down,

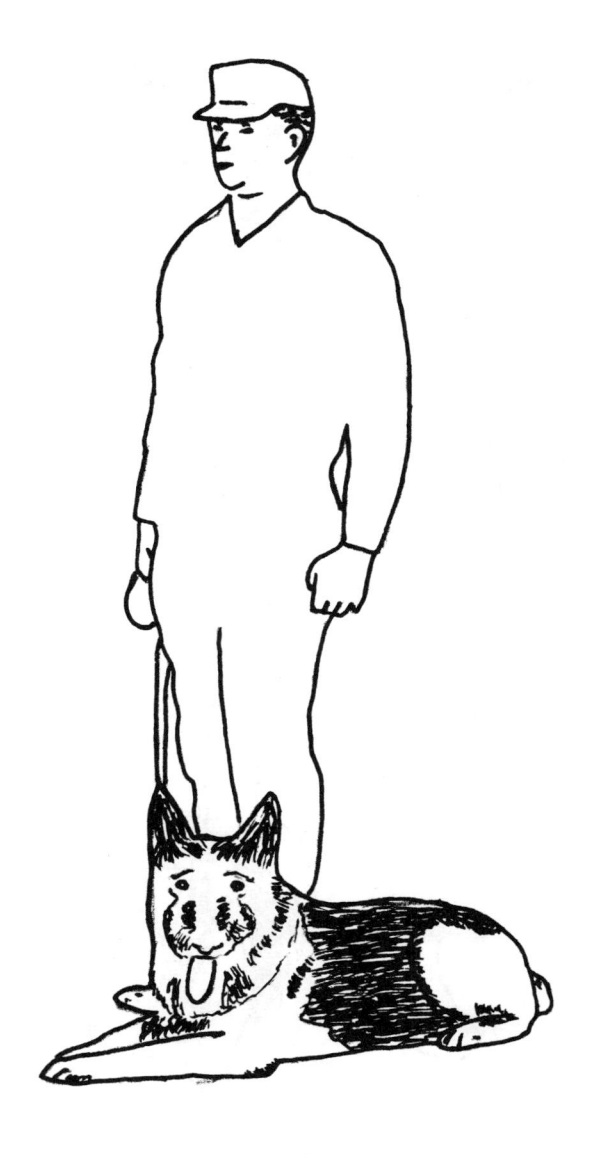

Down position.

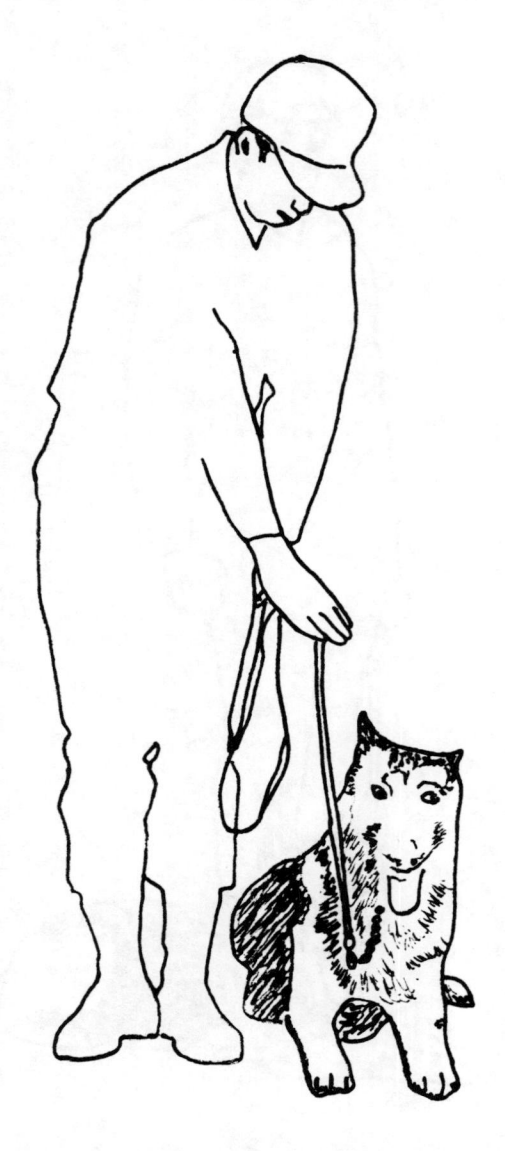

Down hand gesture, handler beside dog.

How to Train a Guard Dog 91

Introduction of down position at end of leash.

Down gesture at end of leash.

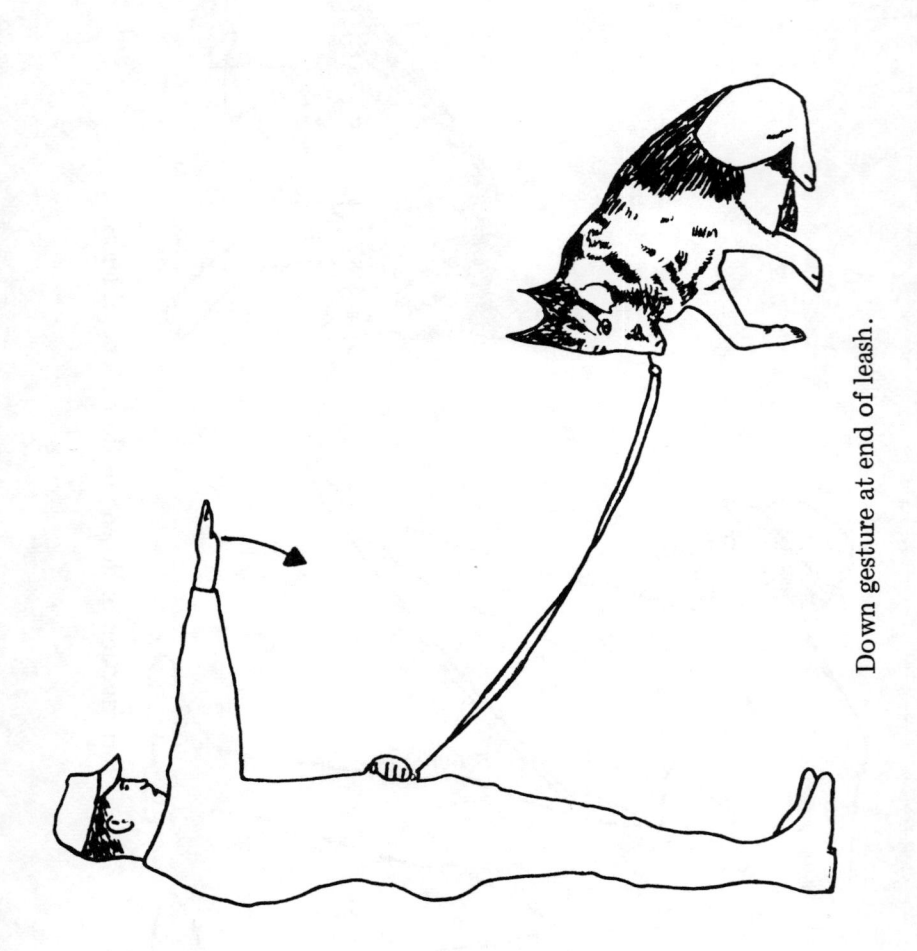

give the gesture and verbal command STAY, and bring your right foot back alongside your left foot. As the dog makes progress, the step-in can be discontinued. Give the command DOWN, and make a sweeping downward gesture with the right hand. Praise the animal when it executes the DOWN position correctly.

Take cover

The command TAKE COVER is not a command to the dog but to yourself. This command is taught to prevent the animal from becoming alarmed or confused when you drop to the ground. This cover action is necessary when you must assume a defensive position to protect yourself.

At the same time you drop to the ground, give the dog the command DOWN. It then goes to the down position as you drop to the ground. When you first practice this exercise, don't drop to the ground too suddenly; if you do this, your dog may become frightened and attempt to jump up. After several trials, it becomes used to this exercise.

Come

The final command taught during basic obedience training is the command COME. The other basic obedience commands, particularly the command STAY, must have been taught and the dog must be performing satisfactorily before you teach it the command COME.

To execute this movement correctly, the dog, upon hearing its name called followed by the command COME and the proper gesture, comes promptly to the heel position at your side.

To begin this exercise, give the command STAY. Stepping off with the right foot, move to the end of the leash and turn to face the dog. Call its name, and follow with the command COME; for example: Duke! COME (during the progression of training calling the dog's name is omitted). As you call and give the command COME, tug lightly on the leash to suggest the meaning of the command. Change the end of the leash to your right hand and give the command HEEL.

During the early stages of this exercise, you may be more effective in teaching this command if you used the following method. As the dog advances, step back with your left foot, grasp the other end of the leash with your left hand, and guide the dog around and into the heel position. When it is in the heel position, stand next to it and give the command SIT.

Crawl

On the command CRAWL, the dog is either beside or facing towards you. (This movement is useful if you come under fire.) When first teaching a dog to crawl, don't lie down beside the animal because it could become irritated and might snap at your face. Instead, kneel down in front of the dog and make it crawl toward you by pulling on the leash.

While pulling on the leash, use the hand gesture for CRAWL, which is done by waving the hand from side to side in front of the dog's face. If it tries to rise, pull down and forward on the choke chain and at the same time give the command CRAWL.

When the dog becomes good at crawling, stand facing it at a distance of several feet and give the oral command and hand gesture to crawl.

When it has progressed satisfactorily in this phase of training you can give the command DOWN and then lie down beside it; now you start crawling, at the same time giving the command CRAWL, and encouraging the animal to crawl beside you.

After teaching the basic commands HEEL, NO, SIT, STAY, DOWN, TAKE COVER, COME, and CRAWL, you are ready to advance to the next phase of training, intermediate obedience training.

How to Train a Guard Dog

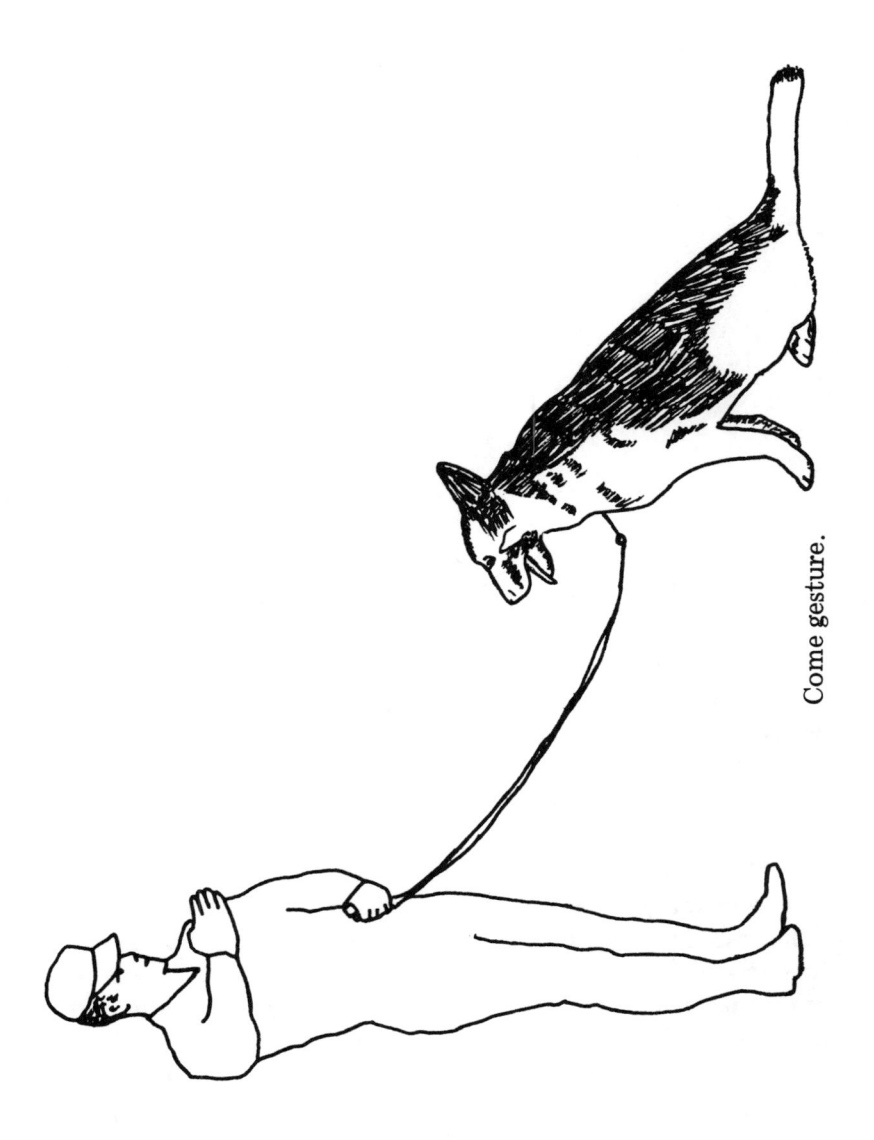

Come gesture.

Intermediate Training

Intermediate obedience training consists primarily of teaching the dog to be obedient while the handler is at the end of the 300-inch training leash. Obedience at an obstacle course is also part of this training.

Commands from a distance

The primary objective of the training is to further develop the control which you have over your dog. It must be taught to execute all the basic commands at a distance. The techniques used with the leather leash can be used with the 300-inch web training leash. If the dog does not react properly to commands while on the 300-inch leash, return to the use of the 60-inch leash. Patience and repetition are necessary when conducting this type of training.

Initially, it will be difficult to train your dog to stay in any given position while you may be as much as 25 feet away. When you go more than 4 or 5 feet beyond the animal, it may have a tendency to break position. This is natural, because it has developed a liking for you and may want to follow you. Repeat all exercises until you have complete control over the dog; this requires patience.

Place your dog in a line when conducting obedience training from the end of the 300-inch leash. It must be taught to sit and to lie down when given the appropriate vocal command or hand gesture. Both are used simultaneously in the beginning, but as training progresses, the dog is taught to react separately to either the vocal command or the hand gesture. Usually, it is best to train the animal in distant obedience for a while and then work it on the confidence course.

Confidence course

Most security dogs perform strenuous duty; because of this, don't expect your dog to maintain maximum proficiency unless it is in top physical condition. In addition to receiving proper food and medical care, it must be exercised frequently and regularly. However, you must consider your dog's age and physical ability before you can design a proper exercise program.

A confidence course provides an excellent medium for exercise. The use of such a course aids you in developing control over your dog, and builds its self-confidence. In order to be beneficial, the course should contain several different types of obstacles. (Of course, if such a course is not available you can use local parks and school fields for training. For example, park benches could be used as obstacles.)

Almost any dog can jump a 3-foot hurdle. Because of the

defensive dog's size, this is not too difficult; the purpose of this training is to get the animal to jump on command.

At this stage of training, the dog has been taught to walk in the heel position at your side. The command used during this exercise is HUP. Upon hearing this command, the dog jumps or scales the obstacles and then returns to your side in the heel position.

The dog may have been taught to jump over hedges or other obstacles but may be afraid of a hurdle. For this reason, it is often advisable to start this exercise using a hurdle that is low enough for the animal to walk over.

Begin this exercise by stepping over the hurdle with your left foot, while simultaneously giving the command HUP. If the dog hesitates or balks, stop on the far side and coax or help it over by tugging on the leash. After it successfully crosses the hurdle, step away from it, praise the animal, and give the command HEEL.

This exercise is continued until the dog can walk or jump over the hurdle without help. When it clears the initial height, higher obstacles can be used until a height of not more than 3 feet has been obtained.

By the time the higher obstacles are attempted, the dog should be so proficient in the execution of the command HUP that you need not continue to step over the hurdle with it; instead, you should pass around the hurdle on the right side. The leash is slack and in your left hand. As you pass the hurdle, give the command HUP. If this procedure is followed, the dog will soon learn to jump over the hurdle when given the command HUP before passing the hurdle.

It is important that practice in jumping and scaling not be overdone in any one period. Although the animal may enjoy these exercises, they are very tiring. In determining the length of these exercises, you must consider your dog's age and weather conditions. Don't overwork a dog during hot weather. A young dog can stand longer and more rigorous training exercises than an older animal. Specific instructions can be obtained from a veterinarian as to what training on the confidence course old dogs and dogs with medical problems should receive.

When a dog is taught to crawl through a tunnel, it is usually necessary for its handler to assist it. It can be walked to the end of the tunnel to examine it; then hold the leash close to the snap, coil the remainder of the leash, and throw it through the tunnel. Attach the snap to the choke chain, put the dog in the down position, and command it to STAY. Move to the other end of the tunnel, look through it so the dog can see you, and coax it through. If necessary tug on the leash; this indicates to the animal that you want it to come through the tunnel. The commands COME and CRAWL may also be used during initial training.

After the dog has accomplished this exercise, it is praised and the exercise is repeated until your assistance is no longer required.

When teaching a dog to walk along a log or ladder, stay close to its side and continuously encourage it. If it jumps off before completing the walk, praise it for having walked that far; then the exercise is undertaken again. The animal will soon gain confidence in its ability to walk over the obstacle and does so while you walk along near or beside it.

Caution must be used during this exercise. Before it begins, the log or ladder is checked to determine its condition. If they are wet or slippery, dry them to prevent injury to the animal.

When the dog is completely obedient and correctly executes the commands it is given from a distance, and when it boldly traverses the confidence course without error, the objectives of the intermediate phase of obedience training have been accomplished. You can then proceed to the advanced phase of obedience training.

Advanced Training

The purpose of advanced obedience training is to gain complete control over your dog. You must have this control over the animal during the performance of the more extreme and dangerous field problems and security duties.

Off-leash obedience training

This type of training is conducted by working the dog off-leash and at varying distances from yourself. All commands taught in basic and intermediate obedience training are used.

If any difficulty is encountered during this phase of training, return immediately to the use of the 300-inch training leash. Because the dog is off-leash, it is absolutely essential that all commands be obeyed without hesitation.

To prevent the possibility of dog fights during the initial phase of this training (if using a public place for training) a good procedure is to muzzle the animal. This procedure, however, should be discontinued as soon as possible because it is distracting to the dog.

Agitation

Advanced agitation training consists of agitating the dog to the extent of making it bite at the agitator. The agitator wears an attack sleeve to give the dog something to actually bite. He uses a stick or burlap bag to agitate the animal, and builds the dog up by acting frightened and backing away every time it advances. Without exception the dog must always be the winner. A trainer/owner or handler never agitates his own dog.

The dog should always wear the leather collar for agitation training. As soon as a session has been completed this collar is removed; in this way the animal soon comes to associate the leather collar with agitation and when it is placed around its neck it will begin to search for an agitator. The dog also wears the leather collar while performing sentry duty. It is important that this (leather) collar-agitator association be established early and firmly. The choke chain is used only when taking the dog to or from the kennel area and during obedience training.

It is agitation which develops the aggressiveness and viciousness essential to an effective guard dog. Its agressiveness and viciousness determine its alertness on post and urge to attack. It is important to keep in mind that each dog is an individual with a distinct temperament of its own, and to obtain the best results, agitation must be suited to the dog. There are three principal methods of agitation.

Line agitation

If more than one dog is being trained line agitation can be

used. You will also need several persons to help you. To begin line agitation handlers and dogs form a single line at intervals of about 15 feet, the dogs standing at HEEL. The agitator quietly approaches one end of the line from the rear. He stops when he is about 30 feet from the first dog and handler. The first dog and handler advance slowly toward the agitator. The handler incites his dog with the command WATCH HIM. When the dog comes to within 10 feet of him, the agitator acts excited and afraid and begins to retreat, walking backwards. The dog is allowed to approach within 3 feet of the agitator who then agitates it a few moments with his stick, while continuing to retreat.

The handler then calls off his dog and leads it back to the other end of the agitation line while the next dog and handler start the same procedure. This should continue until each dog has gone through three repetitions with the agitator. The dog is not allowed to take hold of the agitator during this exercise.

Several naturally aggressive dogs are brought out at the same time. These are dogs which have demonstrated that they do not need to be chained to a stake. Between every two of these animals place a dog that has reacted negatively to the first phase of training. All dogs are lined up far enough apart so that they cannot get into a fight among themselves.

Each dog is on a leash at the left side of the handler. The command WATCH HIM is given when the agitator appears and walks toward the dogs. Some of the dogs will bark immediately; these should be praised by their handlers. The agitator concentrates his attention on the dogs that do not respond readily. He approaches them with his stick, threatens them, and jumps away. Inspired by the bolder dogs beside them, even the slow ones will eventually start barking.

If properly encouraged by their handlers, they will understand that there is nothing to fear from the agitator, and that he will disappear as soon as they bark, growl, or make a move toward him. When all the dogs alert as soon as the agitator appears, he must vary his direction of approach and increase the distance at which he first appears. The dogs that detect him earliest are praised lavishly.

It will be found that the slower dogs learn from their aggressive companions, as well as from their handlers. Overaggressive dogs SHOULD NOT be used in line agitation.

When all the dogs in the class alert at the approach of the agitator, a new man takes his place. The dog learns in this way that any man approaching is an enemy. It is desirable to have numerous persons play the role of the agitator, dressed in different clothing.

You must now play the role of a sentry, walking post with your dog heeling on loose leash. When you and the animal have advanced a short distance, the agitator approaches from some place of concealment. If the dog has learned its first lesson, it will detect the approach of the agitator and will alert you without help. If the animal does not alert you, give it the cue by commanding WATCH HIM. As soon as the dog gives warning, the agitator runs out of sight and you should praise and encourage the dog.

If the dog does not respond correctly, the agitator conceals himself along the animal's path, steps out quickly from his hiding place, hits at the dog with a stick, and jumps away. This will arouse the dog; furthermore, it will learn that unless it gives alarm immediately upon detecting the presence of a stranger, it will be corrected.

When the dog detects and alerts to the presence of all strangers at a considerable distance without any help during the daytime, it is generally ready to be worked at night. It will usually be found that a dog is better at night because scenting conditions are more favorable and its keen hearing is enhanced by the absence of distracting noises.

Stake agitation

Stake agitation follows line agitation. The dog is chained to a tree, post, or stake in some open space away from its kennel. This exercise tends to further build the animal's confidence in itself in unfamiliar places. Some dogs are naturally aggressive and do not need much agitation to become excited.

To avoid accidents, training to arouse aggressiveness may be started by tying the dog to a stake with a kennel chain attached to the broad leather collar. It is advisable to loosen an inch or two of the earth around the stake so that it will give a little when the dog lunges, and not check it too sharply. Heel the dog to the end of the chain, order it to sit and step away.

When the agitator approaches and comes within sight put the dog on the alert by the command WATCH HIM, uttered in a low voice, almost a whisper. This command is used only during early training. It is a signal for the dog that it is on duty and must be prepared to detect any intrusion. The command should be eliminated as soon as the animal has learned that putting on the collar and leash signifies that it is on duty. WATCH HIM is never used in actual service to alert the dog; it must alert you of danger, and not the other way around.

The agitator appears, equipped with a small, flexible stick (rolled magazine, newspaper, etc.) or some other harmless weapon. He approaches the dog from an angle, not facing it directly. Looks at the animal out of the corner of his eyes; he does not stare at it. He then strikes at the dog without hitting it and jumps away. As the agitator strikes, encourage your dog by commanding GET HIM, in a sharp voice; dogs will respond to this procedure according to their natural aggressiveness.

Muzzle agitation

This is an exercise for sentry dogs. The dog is muzzled and

allowed to attack its agitator who wears regular clothing. This actually is a test to determine if the animal will attack, on command, persons not dressed in the attack suit. During training, many dogs seem to acquire an almost exclusive association between the attack suit and "enemy". This form of agitation will determine if the animal is "suit happy" or not.

Dogs are never agitated from a vehicle. Eventually this will cause them to look for and react against vehicles instead of people. In addition, they become nervous and excited when vehicles approach, making it difficult to get them to enter one and ride calmly.

Normally, dogs should be agitated at least three times weekly to keep them at the peak of their effectiveness, but the temperament of individual animals should also be considered in determining the amount of agitation they need. Under no circumstances will a dog be agitated without you being present.

Attack training

This training teaches the dog to attack and stop its attack on command. The command to attack is GET HIM and the command to release or stop attacking is OUT. At the command GET HIM, drop the leash and the dog attacks. On the command OUT, the dog releases and watches the intruder. It then returns to you only on command.

Proceed with your dog to an area isolated from both pedestrian and vehicular traffic. In the training area, put the leather work collar on the dog; do not remove it until the exercise is completed. The agitator, dressed in an attack suit, should be concealed upwind from the dog so that his scent will be driven directly into the animal's nose.

For the first exercise in this phase of training, it is important for the agitator to be well-concealed, but within easy scenting distance and directly upwind from the dog. Command SEARCH, the dog should then try to locate the agitator by scent and sound. When the dog alerts and pulls on the leash, put your hand on his flank, stroking it gently and whispering the words "atta boy, good boy" to praise it. Praise the dog enough to encourage it, but don't distract it. Its attention must remain focused in the direction of the agitator.

The dog approaches the concealed agitator; again use words of praise and encouragement. When it is within a short distance from the agitator, he breaks cover. Order him to halt and place his hands over his head; he ignores the order and tries to escape. Release the dog and command GET HIM; the animal then pursues and attacks the agitator who, after a brief struggle, ceases to resist. Approach, command OUT, and draw the dog away from the agitator, at the same time praising and patting it.

Lead the animal about 10 feet away from the agitator and command DOWN, STAY and WATCH HIM. Return to the agitator and search him, being careful never to place yourself between the dog and the agitator. In the course of the search, the agitator strikes or pushes you to the ground and tries to run away. At this point the dog must attack him WITHOUT command from you.

Attacking under gunfire

Attack under gunfire is taught after the dog is well-trained and you are sure that it will obey all commands and gestures to attack and cease to attack. The agitator wears the attack suit. The procedure is like that described in the preceding paragraphs, except that when the dog flushes the agitator, you and he exchange handgun shots (blanks only!), you firing first.

The exercise then continues through all the stages of pursuit, capture, guard and search. When exchanging shots, you and the agitator should be careful to fire up in the air, away from both yourselves and the animal.

Guarding a prisoner

On the command DOWN, the dog assumes this position in front of a motionless "prisoner" in the attack suit. It must not be close enough for the prisoner to injure it with a sudden kick. Command WATCH HIM to put the dog on alert, and walk away to a hiding place where you can observe the dog's actions. The prisoner then starts to turn around, walk, or run away. If the dog does not attack when the prisoner moves, come out immediately and command GET HIM.

This exercise is repeated until the dog pursues and attacks the prisoner whenever he moves. The exercise should always conclude with you returning to the scene, taking charge of the prisoner, and praising the dog.

Escorting a prisoner

The dog is taught that a prisoner is not to be attacked when accompanied by its handler. Training example: The prisoner suddenly turns in a threatening manner or starts to run away. Drop the leash and the dog, if well trained, will attack. At first you may need to command GET HIM.

The procedure is repeated until the dog attacks without command when the prisoner makes any sudden break, but refrains from attacking when he is marching in an orderly manner ahead of you. Praise your animal at the conclusion of each exercise.

Additional training notes

Importance of loose heeling: In walking a post, loose heeling is essential as long as the dog does not pull or tug on the leash. If you insist on close heeling, the dog is more likely to concentrate on perfection in heeling; this means that its attention will be on you and not on the surroundings. It is then likely to forget its main duty, which is to be alert at all times and ready to give alarm at the slightest provocation.

Importance of distrust of strangers: The guard dog is taught not to make friends with strangers. Training examples: Walk your dog on leash at the heel position. A stranger approaches uttering soothing words and coaxes the dog to come to him; as soon as the animal starts to respond with friendliness, the stranger slaps it smartly on the nose and jumps away; you should then encourage the dog to attack him. This is repeated with different people acting as strangers until the dog growls and barks on the approach of all strangers, no matter how friendly their attitude or how much they attempt to appease the animal.

Next, a stranger tries to entice the dog with a piece of meat or any other bit of food. If the dog tries to take the food, the stranger slaps it on the nose and runs away without giving it the food. In this way the dog learns that you are the only person to be trusted.